A Collec
Curious Jujutsu
Manuals
Volume II

Annotated Translations of five works from the:

1600–1868   1868–1912   1912–1926
E d o · Meiji · Taisho

シャハン・エリック 訳

TRANSLATED BY ERIC SHAHAN

Translator's Introduction

In the Edo Era 1603-1868 Samurai martial arts families made their living working for the government in each of the Domains of Japan. After the Meiji Restoration in 1868 these hereditary warriors lost their primary source of income and had to rely on paying students or seek employment. However, since the "modern era" had begun many people were inclined to leave the study of military matters to the army or navy. This resulted in many martial arts schools closing due to a lack of students. Other schools attempted to stave off closure by repackaging their ideas as general self-defense. This meant paring down the normally large curricula and focusing on (what the authors considered to be) practical. The other avenue they explored was the recuperative or resuscitative benefits of Jujutsu therapy. The same striking points on the body that are used to topple enemies can also be used to revive people that have been injured, knocked unconscious or drowned. So many former Samurai billed their methods as a kind of "first-aid" that everyone should know. To the modern reader some of these "resuscitation methods" can be rather frightening and serve as a reminder how much rescue techniques have developed.

This is a collection of short volumes on Jujutsu and resuscitation and therapy books that I have read and used as reference material over the past few years. They are all interesting in their own right, however, since some of the books were rather short and others had little to no accompanying text I have not published translations of them. It occurred to me to make a compilation of all of these shorter volumes to make them available to the many people interested in early texts on Jujutsu, Jujutsu therapy and the development of mass market self-defense manuals that occurred after the Meiji Restoration. Included in this work are two manuals on Jujutsu from the Edo Era. While these manuals are extensively illustrated they contain almost no accompanying text. While the Meiji Era books are strictly translations, I provide my own descriptions for the illustrations in the Edo Era books. These are strictly my opinion of what the illustrations are depicting, intended to give the reader one possible interpretation. These interpretations are based on my years of practicing traditional Japanese martial arts, both Jujutsu and with weapons.

In addition most of the books talked about the importance of self-defense since crime soared in the lawless days immediately following the restoration. I decided to investigate some of the major assaults that occurred in the Edo and Meiji Eras to give a sense of what kind of violence existed.

Overall, I'm really impressed with these little books. No matter how silly some of the techniques may be, there is always some little gem of knowledge hidden within them.

Thank You!
I would like to express my sincere gratitude to Lance Gatling for looking over this manuscript.

Notice and Caution!
    The works in this volume are being translated for historical research purposes. Do not attempt to use, employ or try any of these techniques.

Excerpt from:

Shin-shin Shuyo Bujutsu Gokui Tanren Ho

A Method of Training the Body and Mind in the Inner Mysteries of Martial Arts

森野雪男
By Morino Yukio

Published
1916

武術極意體錬法

■ 稽古衣の注意

上衣と、下穿と、帶この三つを一揃ひとして稽古着と云ふのである。

近來、上衣の袖の短かひのを好むで着るが、それは餘り感心しない。稽古の時には、非常の便宜でもある代り、姿勢に於て、不便此上も無い見苦しいものである。

上衣は、白木綿で、包袖の袷せ襦袢に作り、白糸を振つて、横に細かに刺すのである。そして上衣包袖は、成るたけ長くつくるのを宜しとする。肱よりは二寸長く縫ふのである。

10

Notes and Cautions Regarding the Keiko-gi, Training Gear

The Keiko-gi consists of three parts the Uwagi (top,) Shita Haki (pants) and the Obi (belt.)

Recently there is a trend towards Keiko-gi with shorter sleeves, however, I don't recommend that type. While they are very convenient for training, they tend to encourage bad posture and makes witnessing such training painful.

The Uwagi should be white cotton short-sleeved shirt sewn on top of a straight-sleeved Juban undershirt. Attach these by sewing horizontal rows of fine stitching with white thread. When making this ensure that the overall length as well as the sleeves are long enough. Sew the sleeves so they extend 2 Sun (6 centimeters) past the elbows.

Every part of the Keiko-gi has a name; see the illustrations on the following pages.

Translator's note: This excerpt details how a Keiko-gi (now commonly referred to as a "Gi") should be constructed and the reasoning behind its design. It is interesting how it's basically two shirts sewn together and even at this early stage, instructors had an eye for consistency in training gear.

Illustration 1
Keiko-gi no Uwagi: Training Gear Top

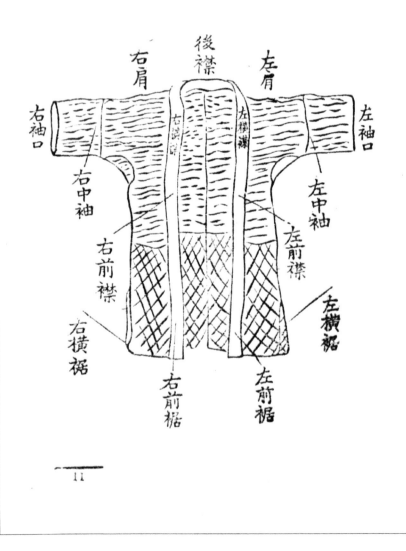

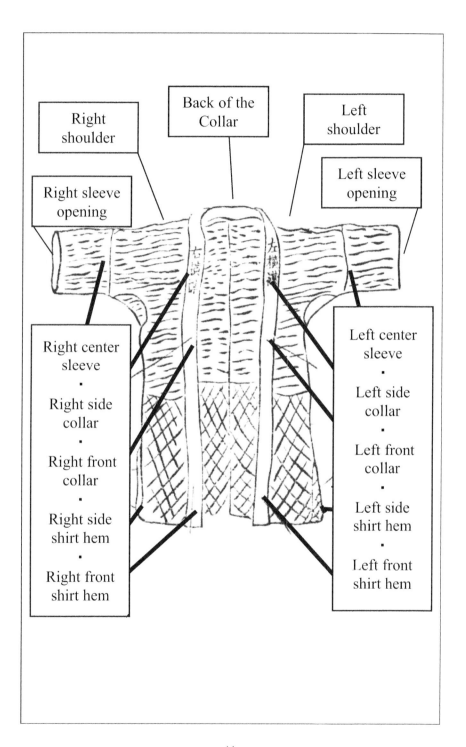

Illustration 2
Keiko-gi no Se: Back of the Training Gear Top

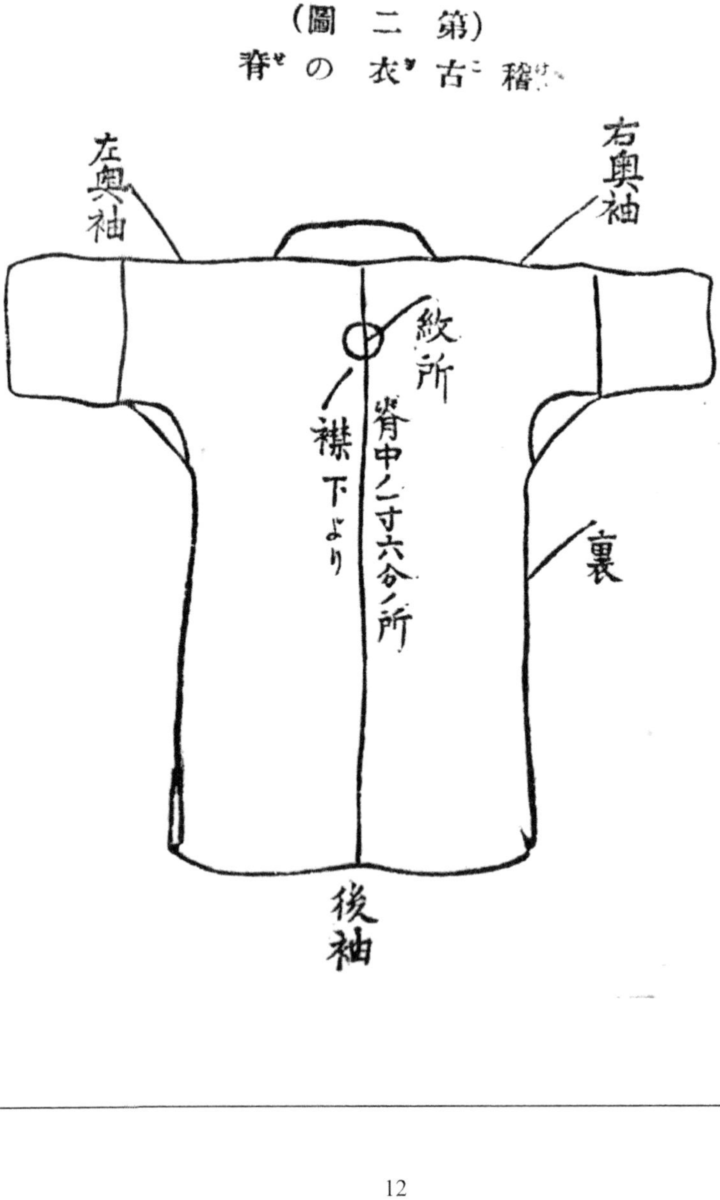

（第　二　圖）
稽こ古こ衣ぎの脊せ

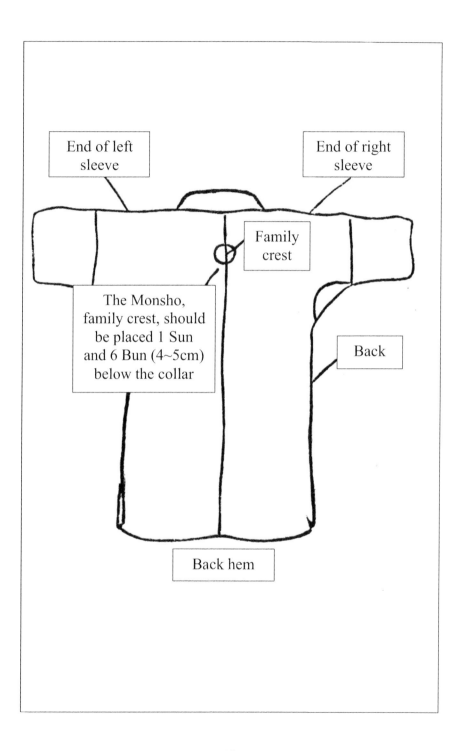

End of left sleeve

End of right sleeve

Family crest

The Monsho, family crest, should be placed 1 Sun and 6 Bun (4~5cm) below the collar

Back

Back hem

柔術膽練法

稽古衣には、各部に名稱が附されてある、それは、鬪に就いて見らし度い。

稽古衣の上衣が前記した通り。肘より短かいのが現代の上衣なのである。否、流行されて在る。

之は、商人等の布地を惜むのと、稽古する者が勝手を爭ふ際に四本の指先を兩袖口へ入れて、握りやすいのを喜ぶからだ。それが仕業の技と防禦とに便利なので、短かいの〵のと好み出したのだ。然し、之れは大なる弊害なのである。

尤も修業後ならば、如何なる持方や着衣でも差支へは無いが、初心者にはあまり感心されない持方と上衣である。第一危險と云

13

The upper Keiko-gi is as shown on the previous page. Modern Keiko-gi tend to have sleeves that end above the elbows. Well it is probably more correct to say that is the fashion these days. Part of this is a mercantile desire to save money on fabric, however those who train in Jujutsu regularly like the short sleeves because the first four fingers of each hand can easily slide into the sleeve and grip.

Since this is an advantage when applying techniques or defending, short sleeves have become popular, however there is a significant downside to this fad. While practitioners who have trained extensively can grip anywhere on any type of clothing, a beginner will have a great deal of difficulty adapting their grip to different types of clothing.

武術極意腦練法

はねばなら無い、
何故ならば、自
然防禦の方に重
きをおき、姿勢
が防禦のみに偏
するうれいがあ
る。それに、體
の働が不充分で
技の發達上に少
からぬ障害があ

（第 三 圖）

稽古衣の腹帶

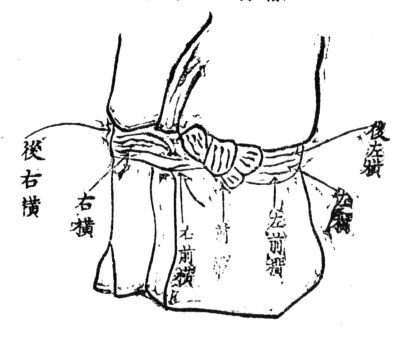

後左襟

後右横

右横

右前襟

前

左前襟

14

This is the biggest downside to using a Keiko-gi with short sleeves. Further, there is a natural tendency for beginners to defend and rely on defensive strategies rather than attack. This limits the range of techniques a beginner can learn and hinders progress towards a higher level of proficiency.

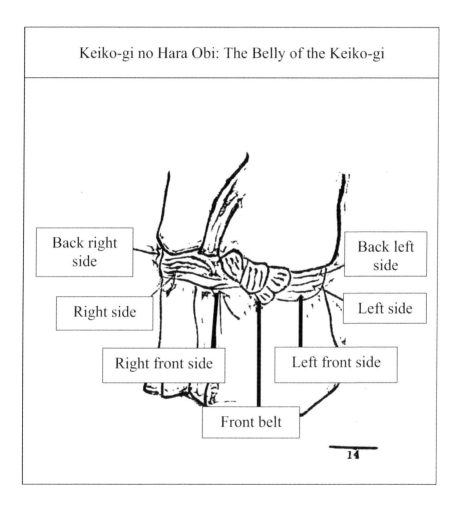

Keiko-gi no Hara Obi: The Belly of the Keiko-gi

柔術鵬練法

（第四圖）

稽古衣の下穿

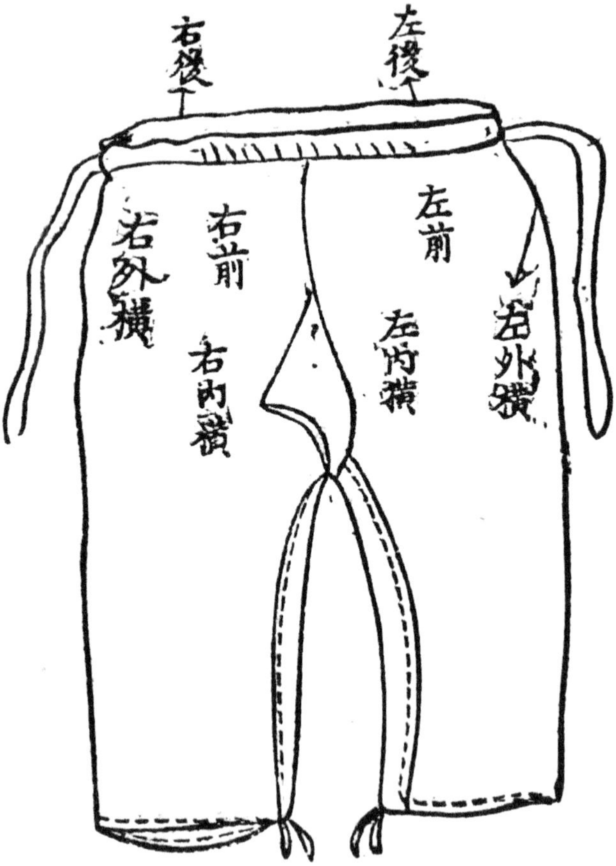

右後　左後

右外横　右前　左前　右外横

右内横　左内横

15

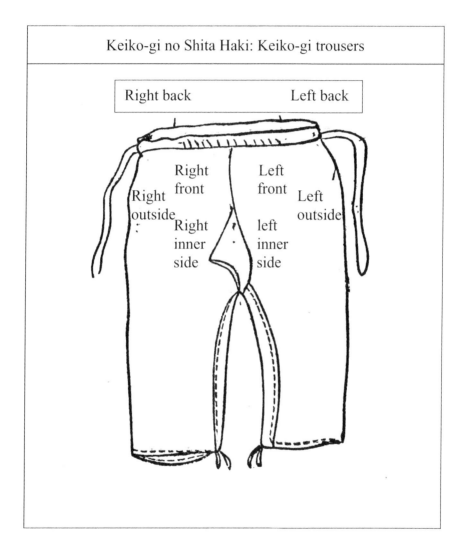

Keiko-gi no Shita Haki: Keiko-gi trousers

武術極意膽練法

るのだ。

柔術の應要の時に、相手が縦令裸體だらうが、どんな着衣だら

うと、それに應ずる修業をして置かねばなら無い技、稽古衣は成

る可く、一般に用ひらるゝやう作られたいのである。と云つて、

俄かに改良も出來まいから、なるたけ稽古衣の袖は、長くつくら

れて欲しいのである。肱より二三寸位にして、袖口も拳の入るぐ

らゐにされたいと云ふのである。

For Jujutsu it doesn't matter what clothing an opponent wears, or if he is completely naked. Jujutsu principles are applied in the same way. However, in order for you to learn how to apply Jujutsu against an opponent wearing any sort of clothing you must learn how to apply techniques effectively, therefore your Keiko-gi should be made in a standard fashion.

It is my opinion that even small adjustments should be avoided in favor of a Keiko-gi with long sleeves. The sleeves should extend 2 or 3 Sun (6 ~7 cm) below the elbow, with the sleeve opening large enough to allow a person's fist to pass through.

起倒
雄心

柔術秘傳解

Full text of:

Kito Yushin Jujutsu Hiden Kai

An Explanation of the Secret Jujutsu Techniques of the Kito Yushin School

Author Unkown
Published 1905

An Explanation of the Secret Jujutsu Techniques of the Kito Yushin School

Author Unkown
Published Meiji 38
1905

一柔術秘傳ハ方今世上ニ行ル、如キ只
々柔術ノ形影ヲ知ルニ止マラズ秘傳
ノ深奥ヲ探リ筆紙ノ盡ス克ハザル處
ノ活術奇法ヲ一々平易ノ俗語ヲ以テ
解キ且ッ精密ナル術ヲ顯シ奇々至妙
ノ奥秘ナル故身躰ノ肥痩強弱長短ハ
論ナク我ガ意ノ如ク心ノ想フマ、ニ
人ヲ自由自在ニ起倒轉伏死活セシム
ナレバ平素此術ヲ研練セバ身躰ノ健
保ナルハ活目シテ看ルベキナリ諸士
一讀ヲ乞フ稱讚シ併テ秘傳柔術ノ秘
術ニ感服アランヿヲ希テ止ズト云爾

Kito Oshin Jujutsu Hiden Kai
An Explanation of the Secret Jujutsu Techniques of the Kito Yushin School

One

It seems like of late everywhere you go you encounter the topic of Jujutsu Hiden, Secrets of Jujutsu. However, the information being transmitted by many of these sources is only a shadow of the real Jujutsu. In order to reveal the true inner mysteries of this art I have taken brush to paper and exerted serious effort.

Some of the techniques are practical and some are quite mysterious, however they will all be described in clear understandable language. Moreover, the explanation of the techniques will be detailed enough to allow the reader to grasp the meaning of the inner mysteries of these techniques. You will become able to direct your will and your spirit despite your fatness, thinness, strength, weakness, adeptness or cleverness. You will become able to collapse, throw, kill or breathe life into your opponent as you see fit.

If you make training these techniques part of your regular life, you will soon, with careful observation, realize your body has become healthy and strong. My one desire is to humbly request all Samurai read this volume and adopt its lessons in the secrets of Jujutsu.

Note:
This book uses many different terms for "opponent." They include:
Warumono – Bad Guy
Teki – Enemy
Aite – Opponent

一、柔術ハ武門六藝ノ父母ナリ六藝ト云
ハ弓・馬・劍・槍・砲・銃ノ六種ナリ其中何術
ヲ修業スルニモ此柔術ヲ學ビ置キ此
心得ヲ藝ノ基トスレバ眞ニ其術ヲ早
ク得ルモノナル故ニ他ノ武藝ヲ産出
スルガ如キヲ以テ之ヲ父母ト云フナ
リ今兵士ノ銃ノ撃方ヲナスニ柔軟體
操スルガ如キ又柔術ハ我ガ力ニテ行
フニアラズ柔術ト故能ク我ガ体ヲコ
ナス事其他凡テ習熟スベシ

一、柔術ノ名目ハ豫メ六部門トス
居取・立合・中段・要門居要門柄捌ノ六藝ナリ

Two

Jujutsu is considered to be the "mother and father" of the Six Schools of Martial Arts. The Six Schools of Martial Arts are:

弓 Kyu - Archery
馬 Ba - Equestrian
剣 Ken - Sword Fighting
槍 So - Spear Fighting
砲 Ho - Cannon
銃 Ju - Rifles

No matter which of the above schools of martial arts you seek to study, having a foundation in Jujutsu will allow you to absorb the teachings of another martial art much faster. So, the reason Jujutsu is referred to as the "mother and father of martial arts" is because it gives birth to all others. Even today, soldiers, though they are carrying rifles, rely on a flexible body in order to take their firing positions. However, Jujutsu does not move through force, rather, the fundamental nature of it is to enable people to employ our bodies to the fullest. Thus it is important to strive to train frequently and diligently.

Three

Jujutsu is divided into six categories. The Six Arts of Jujutsu are:

Idori - Techniques done while seated in Seiza
Tachiai - Standing Technqiues
Chudan – Mid-level Techniques
Yomon - Techniques that focus on positioning the hips
I-Yomon - Related to Yomon
Eh-Sabaki - Fighting unarmed against an opponent armed with a sword. You attack the Eh, or handle, of the sword.

Note: The handle of the sword in Japanese is called Tsuka or Eh. The Kanji is the same 柄.

一柔術ノ奥秘ヲ知ラント欲セバ先ヅ第
一二中身急所ヲ知ルベシ故ニ其大略
ノ急所ヲ左ニ示ス

Four

If you wish to become knowledgeable about the Oh-hi, Inner Secrets, of Jujutsu the first thing you need to familiarize yourself with is Atemi and Kyusho. Atemi are Striking Points and Kyusho are Vital Points. See the abbreviated Kyusho chart below. Note:

The following illustrations show Kyusho and Atemi points. Kyusho means "vital point" and Atemi means "striking point." In Jujutsu these points serve as targets to inflict the most amount of damage. Conversely they were also be used to resuscitate a person who has fallen unconscious, drowned or become injured. Each Kyusho has Kanji, however the readings for these are not given so the names as well as the meanings are approximate. Only someone well versed in this school would know the full meaning of each term.

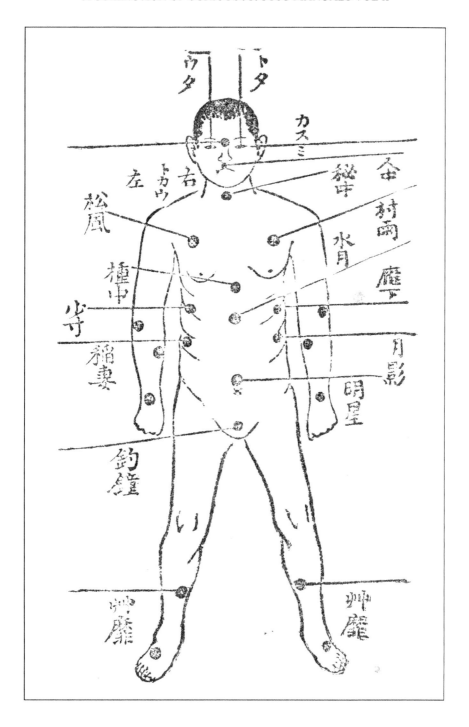

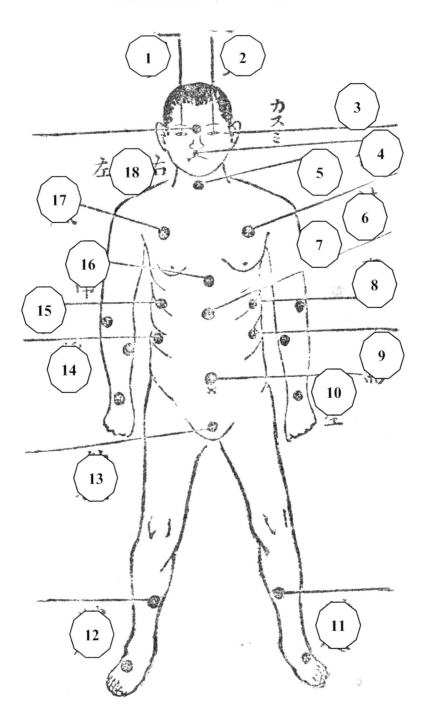

#	Approximate Japanese Reading	(Meaning of Japanese) Body Part
①	Uta	Right Eye
②	Tota	Left Eye
③	Kasumi	(Mist) Temple
④	Jinchu	(Center of Man) Spot below the nose
⑤	Hichu	(Center of the Secret) Adam's apple
⑥	Murasame	(Village Rain) Left Chest
⑦	Suigetsu	(Moon reflected on Water) solar plexus
⑧	Nagishita	(Bent Below) Last rib on the left
⑨	Tsukikage	(Shadow of the Moon) liver
⑩	Meisei	(Bright Star) Lower Abdomen
⑪	Kusanagi	(Wind blowing grass) Inside of the calf
⑫	Kusanagi	(Wind blowing grass) Inside of the calf
⑬	Tsurukame	(Hanging Bell) testicles
⑭	Inazuma	(Lightning) Kidney
⑮	Shosun	(Just before) Last rib on the right
⑯	Shunaka	(Center of the Seed) Sternum
⑰	Matsukaze	(Pine tree bending in the wind) Right Chest
⑱	Tokau	(Left and right Tokau) Eyebrows

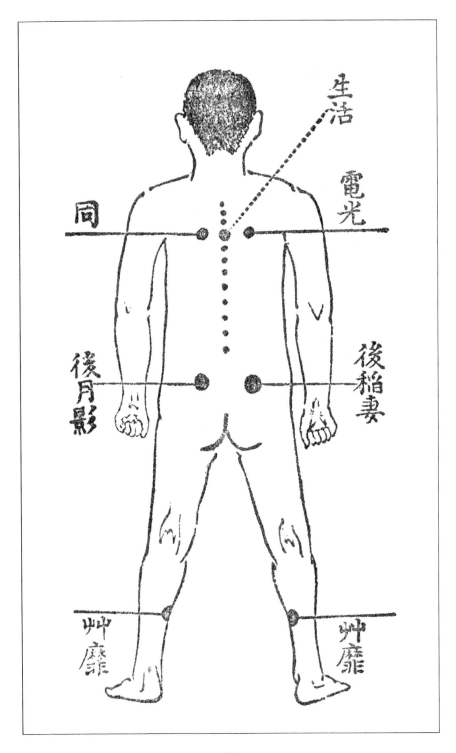

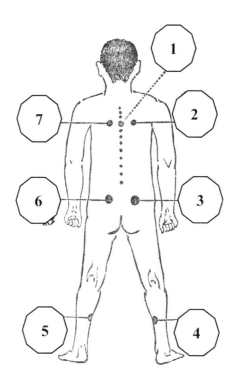

#	Approximate Japanese Reading	(Meaning of Japanese) Body Part
①	Seikatsu	(Life-giving) Resuscitation Point
②	Denko	(Bolt of lightning) Right shoulder blade
③	Ushiro Inazuma	(Lightning on the back) Top of the hip bone
④	Kusanagi	(Wind blowing grass)
⑤	Kusanagi	(Wind blowing grass)
⑥	Ushiro Tsukikage	(Shadow of the moon on the back) Top of the hip bone
⑦	Denko	(Bolt of Lightning) Left shoulder blade

一人躰急所々在中重大ナルハ左ノ四ケ

所ナリ之レヲ俗ニ死活ト云フ

一水月所謂水落ヲ指ス

一松風所謂右肺臓ヲ指ス

一村雨所謂左肺臓ヲ指ス

一人中所謂鼻ノ眞下ヲ指ス

右四ケ所ニ参考ノ為メ左ニ示ス

一水月ハ急所中ノ最モ重大ナルモノナ

レバ各自ニ保護スベシ但シ水月ヲ強

衝スルトキハ蘇生ノ見込ナシ松風、村雨

モ全様ナリ

Five

The four most important Kyusho on the human body are listed below. These are also commonly referred to as Shikatsu, resuscitation points, used to help revive those knocked unconscious.

- Suigetsu - Moon reflected on water. More commonly known as the solar plexus
- Matsu Kaze - Wind in the Pine Trees. More commonly known as (the point on top of) the right lung.
- Mura Same - Rain Passing Over a Village. More commonly known as (the point on top of) the left lung.
- Jin Chu - Center of a man. The place directly under the nose.

I have highlighted these four points in order to emphasize their importance.

Six

The Kyusho called Suigetsu, Moon Reflected on Water, is the most important of the striking points, therefore special care should be taken to note its location. You should be aware that a strong blow to this point will result in so much damage that resuscitation will prove impossible. This applies to Matsu Kase, Wind in the Pine Trees, as well as Mura Same, Rain Passing Over a Village.

第一條　惡者ガ前ヨリ向ヒ來ルヽキハ其
儘ニ後ニ倒スルニハ右足ノ親指ヲ敵
ノ右足ノ跟ニ懸ケ我足ノ節ノ所ニテ
敵ノ向ヅネヲ押シ同一ニ右手ニテ喉
ヲ押スベシ

第二條　惡者ガ胸グラヲ取リ來ルトキ
ハ右左ノ手ニカ、ハラズ其ノ取タル
手ノ甲ヲ手ヲ横ニシテ打ツベシ

Techniques

#1

If you are suddenly beset by a Warumono, a bad person, who lunges straight at you, respond by toppling them backwards. Do this by hooking the big toe of your right foot behind the heel of the opponent's right foot. Use your ankle to push the front of the Warumono's shin while shoving his throat with your right hand.

#2

The Warumono grabs your chest lapel. Strike across to the back of his hand with either your right or left hand.

第三條 若シ惡者ガ前ヨリ拳ヲ振リ上ゲ
打込來リタルトキハ左ノ足ヲ前ニ出シ
躰ヲ斜ニナシ左手ニテ打込來ル手ヲ
首ヲ握リ（圖ノ如ク）迅速ニ右ノ足ヲ敵
ノ右足ノ外ニ添ヘ
ヘルトドウ時ニ右手ニテ敵ノ喉ヲ
押シ直ニ握リタ
ル手ヲ斜ニ引キ
敵ノ足ニ添ヘタル
足ヲ横ニ蹴ベシ

#3

This technique is in response to a Warumono raising his fist and
punching you. Step forward with your left foot and twist your body
diagonally. Grab the wrist of the arm that is punching with your left
hand. Rapidly plant your right foot against his right foot. At the
same time push his throat with your right hand. This is shown in the
illustration. Then immediately pull the attacker's right arm
diagonally downward as you kick his right leg out to the side with
your right foot.

第四條　悪者後ヨリ手ト共ニ抱キ付タ
ルキハ頭ラニテ敵ノ人中ヲ打チ仝時
ニ腰ヲ下リ右手ヲ上ニ左手ヲ下ニノ
バシ躰ヲカハスベシ

#4

    In this situation the Warumono grabs you from behind pinning both arms. Respond by whipping your head back and striking him in Jinchu, the spot below the nose. Next, drop your hips down while raising your right hand and dropping your left arm. This will enable you to twist your body out and escape.

38

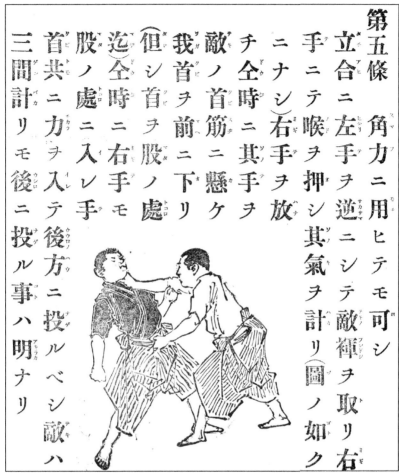

#5

You can also use Jujutsu in conjunction with Sumo. When facing off, grab the bottom of the enemy's Fundoshi, loincloth, with your left hand, palm up. With your right hand push on his throat. You anticipate that he will knock your right arm away. This is shown in the illustration. In response, you immediately grab the side of his neck as you drop your head forward and down, making sure your head is even with your opponent's thighs. At the same time slip your right arm between his thighs. Put power in both your right arm and left wrist and flip the enemy over behind you. The opponent will surely be thrown at least 3 Ken, or about 5.5 meters (1 Ken 間 is about 1.8 meters.)

39

第六條　敵左右ヨリ我両手ヲ取タルニ
其ノ手ヲ放ッニハ我手ヲ上ニ引ヨセ
カヲ入テ下ルト全時ニ前ニ引クベシ

#6

This technique is used when the Teki, enemy, grabs both your left and right wrists at the same time. To free yourself, bring your hands up and together. Put all your power in your hands and then yank your hands down and forward.

第七條 敵前後ヨリ出來リ一人ハ前ヨ
リ打チ掛リ一人ハ後ヨリ我手ト共ニ
抱キ付タルトキハ頭ヲ上ゲテ敵ノ人中ニ
ヲ打チ全時ニ（圖ノ如ク）左手ニテ敵ノ
右手ヲ取リ又全
時ニ我ガ右手ヲ
上テ敵ノ首筋ノ
處ニ掛ケ（最モ此
時ハ充分ニ躰ヲ
下ナリ）力ヲ入テ
前ノ一人ノ敵ニ
投附ルルナリ

#7

In this situation there are two Teki, enemies, one in front and the other behind. The first one approaches you from the front and throws a punch. The second enemy, approaching from behind, grabs you from behind in a bear-hug. Respond by whipping your head back and striking the enemy grabbing you from behind in Jinchu, Center of Man, the spot just below the nose (Kyusho chart #4.) At the same time grab his right arm with your left hand. This is shown in the illustration. With your right hand reach up and grab the enemy's neck. At this point you should drop your hips as low as possible, fill your body with power and throw him forward at the second opponent.

第八條

白刃ヲモチテ我レニ切込來ル
時ハ躰ヲ左リ斜ニナシ敵ニ我躰ヲマ
カシ左手ニテ(第一圖ノ如ク二)受ケ全時
ニ右足ヲ一歩進ミ右手ニテ受ケタル
ニノ右手ノ外ヨリ逆ニ
敵ノ第二圖ノ如ク右足
懸ケ第二圖ノ如ク右足
ヲ敵ノ右足ノ外ニ添へ

第一圖

手足ト共ニ全
時ニ左リノ方
ニ倒スベシ敵
ノ持チタル刀

第二圖

#8

    In this situation the opponent cuts at you with a Hakujin, a white (bared) blade. As he cuts step diagonally to the left, bringing your body in close to the opponent, but out of the line of his cut. Use your left arm to stop the opponent's downward cut. This is shown in illustration one.

    As soon as you stop the cut, step in with your right foot and use your right arm to wrap around the outside of the opponent's right arm. At the same time, slide your right foot against the outside of his right foot. This is shown in illustration two.

    Using your right leg and right arm in unison pull the opponent down on his left side. This should cause him to drop his sword.

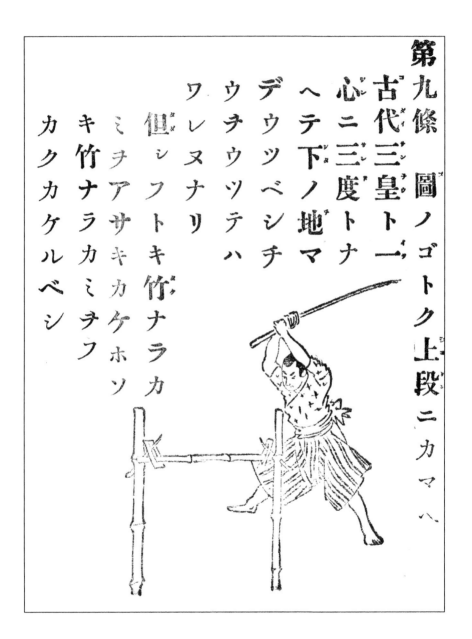

第九條 圖ノゴトク上段ニカマヘハ

古代三皇ト一

心ニ三度トナヘテ下ノ地マ

デウツベシチ

ウヲウツテハ

ワレヌナリ

但レフトキ竹ナラカ

キ竹ナラカミヲフ

カクカケルベシ

ミヲアサキカケホソ

#9 Untitled [How to cut bamboo]

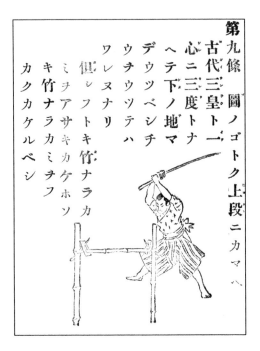

As the illustration shows, stand in Jodan Kamae, Upper Stance, with your sword. Intone three times,
I am one with the Three Sovereign Emperors of old
Then strike down all the way to the ground. If you try to stop halfway, it won't cut. However, if you are attempting to slice thick bamboo, cut towards the tip of the sword. If it is Kake Honki bamboo then cut closer to the base of the blade.

Notes about the Three Sovereigns:
The Three Sovereigns are emperors from prehistoric China. They are said to have existed before 2852 BCE, after which the Five Emperors ruled the earth. The Three Sovereigns were also known as the Three August Ones and used their powers to teach the people things like the use of fire and how to build houses .
Preceding the Three Sovereign Emperors was Pangu 盤古 the first living being in the universe and a creator deity.

In the beginning, there was nothing and the universe was in a formless primordial state. This primordial state coalesced into a cosmic for about 18,000 years. Within it, the perfectly opposed principles of Yin and Yang became balanced, and Pangu emerged from the egg. Pangu then began creating the world: he separated Yin from Yang with a swing of his giant axe, creating the Earth (Yin) and the Sky (Yang). To keep them separated, Pangu stood between them and pushed up the Sky. With each day, the Sky grew 3 meters higher, the Earth 3 meters thicker, and Pangu 3 meters taller. This task took yet another 18,000 years. In some versions of the story, Pangu is aided in this task by the four most prominent beasts, the Turtle, the half-lion half snake Qilin, the Phoenix and the Dragon., After the 18,000 years had elapsed, Pangu died. His breath became the wind, mist and clouds; his voice, thunder; his left eye the Sun; his right eye, the Moon; his head, the mountains and extremes of the world; his blood became the rivers and his muscles the fertile lands. His facial hair became the stars and Milky Way. His fur became forest, his bones became valuable minerals and his bone marrow precious jewels. His sweat became the rain and the fleas on his fur the animals.
Adapted from Wikipedia

James Legge wrote about Pangu in 1881,

P'an-ku is spoken of by the common people as "the first man, who opened up heaven and earth." It has been said to me in "pidgin" English that "he is all the same your Adam"; and in Taoist picture books I have seen him as a shaggy, dwarfish, Hercules, developing from a bear rather than an ape, and wielding an immense hammer and chisel with which he is breaking the chaotic rocks.

From: Legge, James (1881), *The Religions of China: Confucianism and Tâoism Described and Compared with Christianity*, C. Scribner, p. 168.

The **Heavenly Sovereign** 天皇 or *Tiānhuáng* in Chinese was the first of the Three Sovereign Emperors.

According to the Records of the Grand Historian 史記 by Sima Qian 司馬遷 145 – c. 86 BC,

After the Heaven and the Earth were founded, there was Tiānhuáng who had twelve heads, cast his magic to fill the Earth with water. He lived until his age of eighteen thousand.

Translated by Allen, Herbert J. *Chien's Historical Records Journal of the Royal Asiatic Society.* **26** (2): 269–295. 1894.

His greatest achievement was suppressing all the chaos, divided the world to many tribes with choosing the best person to rule his tribe.   The Heavenly Sovereign was succeeded by the Earthly Sovereign.

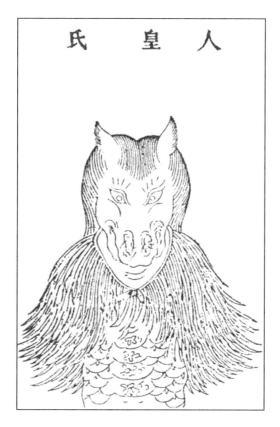

The **Earthly Sovereign** 地皇 or *Dìhuáng* in Chinese was the second of the Three Sovereigns.

According to the Records of the Grand Historian 史記,

Dìhuáng had eleven heads, was the king of Fire…After he was born, the world was filled in chaos. That year, the sun and the moon born from two eyes of Pangu, the stars from his hairs couldn't move smoothly and correctly, which caused many days without sun, or many days with the sun shined all over each day, or many dangerous fallen star accidents. With his power, Dìhuáng corrected the false. He made the sun, the moon move correctly, and stipulated the days of a month, the months of a year. Dìhuáng`s rule lasted eleven thousand years.

Translated by Allen, Herbert J. *Chien's Historical Records Journal of the Royal Asiatic Society.* 1894.

His successor was the Human Sovereign.

The **Human Sovereign** 人皇 or *Rénhuáng* in Chinese was the second of the Three Sovereigns.

According to the Records of the Grand Historian 史記,

*Rénhuáng had seven heads, rode a cloudy chariot, coughed out rice from his mouth. He was of nine brothers. They led **nine provinces**, where each founded his own citadel. Their dynasty ruled through one hundred and fifty (150) generations, lasting forty-five thousand six hundred (45,600) years. His greatest achievement was dividing China into nine provinces, and building the united dynasty lasting forty-five thousand six hundred years.*

Translated by Allen, Herbert J. *Chien's Historical Records Journal of the Royal Asiatic Society*. 1894.

Rénhuáng was the last of the Human Sovereigns. I have never hear of invoking the Three Sovereign Emperors in any other book I have translated with regards to Japanese Martial Arts.

第十條　ノドヲツクヲ
防グ法
一全身ニ力ヲ入レ両手
ヲ堅クニギリ口ヲフ
サギイキヲセズシテ
前ニ押スベシ

#10 How to stop a thrust to your throat.

Fill your body with power and make it rigid. Squeeze your hands into fists. Close your mouth tightly and hold your breath. Push forward into the bamboo.

第十一條　手拭ニテ首ヲシ
ムルヲ防グ法
一全身ニ力ヲ入レ両手
ヲ堅クニギリ口ヲフ
サギ生氣ヲ止テ押ベ
シ

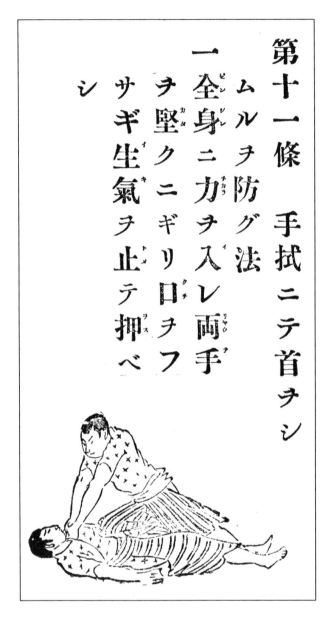

#11 How to defend against being strangled with a Tenugui cloth.

Fill your body with power and squeeze your hands into tight fists. Shut your mouth tightly and hold your breath.

第十二條　小指ニ力

ヲ生ズルノ法

一全身ニ力ヲ入レ右

ノ足ニ充分ニ土ヲ

フミ右ノ親指ニテ

人差指ノフシヲカ

タクニギリ手上ニ

アクヘシ

#12 How to put power in your little finger.

Put power in your whole body. Plant your right foot firmly on the ground. Press your right thumb firmly on the knuckle of your bent index finger and push upward.

第十三條　石ナゲルヲ

防グ法

一両眼ヲ開キ石ヲ
面部ノ中央ニ
（ステーキ）チソ
ナヘ石ノ來ルヲ見テ
オレバ是非ステーキ
二當ルヘシ

#13 How to avoid being hit by rocks.

Keep both eyes open wide. You want the rocks to strike you directly in the face, however you have protected yourself by holding a piece of bamboo there. If you can see the rocks coming at you, you can avoid being struck.

第十四條　小供ニ重
キオ加ヘル法
一小供ヲ直立サセ小
供ノ両手ヲワキノ
シタニ力ヲ入レサ
セテツケ其小供ノ
手平ノ上ハ指二本
下ハ親指ニテカタク二ギ
リ小供ノ手平ニモタルベシ
但シ上ル人ハ小供ノ両ヒヂヨリ上

#14 How to Make a Child Feel Heavy

Have the child stand straight and have him tuck both hands into his armpits and grip tightly. Next take his hands in yours with your thumbs on the bottom of his palms and two fingers on the back of his hands and grip tightly. The person lifting should try and pick the child up from some point above his knees.

第十五條　手平ニス

テーキノック法

一手平ニテ前ニ力ヲ

入レ押スヘシ

但シ取ル人ハ手ヲ

下ヨリ下ニツラシテ取

ルベシ

#15 How to Make Someone's Palm Stick to a Pole

Extend one palm forward and press hard.   The person doing this should be sure to press downward with their hand.

54

第十六條　カラダノオモクナル法
一全身ニ力ヲ入レ右ノ人サシ指ニテ前
ニ押セ

第十七條　此印如三寸ノコ
ヨリデ縛レバ動ケナイ金
シバリ

第十八條　ヤキ火バシシゴク法
東山ノ氷ガ瀧ノ底々ノ水ヲ切テクベ
レバハイトナルランアビラウンケン
ソワカト三度トナヘシゴクベン
是ヲモドスニハ水ニテ手ヲアラウ
コト

#16 How to Make Your Body Heavy

Put power in your whole body and extend your right index finger and push.

#17

If you tie a person up with a piece of Koyori, paper string, as shown in the illustration, they will be unable to move. This is called Kane Shibari, metal tie.

#18 How to Endure Grabbing a Hot Fire Poker

If you chant the following three times before you grab the hot poker you will be able to endure the heat:
[Make this as cold as] *the ice from the eastern mountain is as cool as the bottom-most water of a waterfall.*
Anbira unken 唵阿毘羅吽欠

Once finished you should wash your hands with water to break the spell.

Note: *Anbira unken* is part of a prayer to the Nyorai Buddha.

Jujutsu Gekiken
Hitori Shuho
Hiketsu Zukai

Jujutsu
&
Japanese Fencing:
An Illustrated Guide
to Self-Training

横野鎮次
By Yokono Shizuji

Published
1894

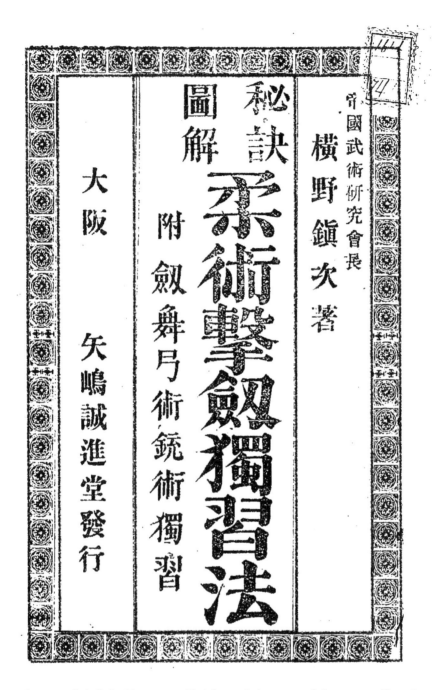

Cover of *A Solo Training Guide to Jujutsu and Japanese Fencing*

58

Translator's Introduction

The illustrations in this book are quite interesting, simultaneously 70's disco and yet somehow there is a pirate vibe. Several of the illustrations show one opponent flexing his body in resistance, was an element of how late 20th century Jujutsu was done. The image on the right is a young Kano Jigoro, the founder of Judo.

柔術獨習法

横野祐光　校閲

横野鎭次　著述

法　秘　術　柔

總論

柔術の由來たるや殆んど空漠にして其確歴を索るの由なし其術を離も其由て來れるの途なくして今日其法は其術を行の理あらざる也中興より足利乱世の時代は武道日に旺盛を極め接戦屢々あり又た術を以て剛を制するあり其劇戦尤も甚し之を以て察するに其當時

Self-Training in Jujutsu
By Yokono Shisuji
Illustrations by Yokono Uko

Introduction

The origins of Jujutsu are rather vague and elusive. Further, there doesn't seem to be any way to truly confirm how it came to be. However, no matter what road the history of Jujutsu traversed to arrive in the here and now, there is both a need and a reason to train in its methods and learn its techniques. What is known is that in the tumultuous 14th~17th centuries, beginning under the Shogun Ashikaga Takauji (1305-1358) Samurai trained continuously in martial arts seeking to perfect their technique. The frequent clashes of that era gave them ample opportunity to learn how to use their methods to control those that were stronger but rigid.

二

よりして業に已に斯術の行はれたるを信ずるに足る

加之ならず武士の要道に於て

柔は剛を制す

ると在り之れ則ち剛を制するの術は柔術なり此に於

て乎柔術の由來たるも亦近きにあらざることを信ず

べきなり

抑も柔術なるものは能く剛を制し屈せざるを挫き敵

せざる力を撃つ所謂自己直接の護身術也故に古來よ

りし此の術に長じたるの士も鶖し然りと雖も他術と

異なるを以て常に心裏胸中に之を藏す之を以て世上

When considering that time and the dramatic battles that occurred, there is no doubt that it was during this period Jujutsu began to be used extensively. The art of Jujutsu soon became an essential tool of the Samurai of that era. The philosophy was,

The soft and flexible can overcome the strong and rigid

This is the origin of Jujutsu.

The fundamental use of Jujutsu is to break enemies that rely exclusively on strength and rigidity by using their own power against them. It is a method of defending yourself when physically attacked. Thus from days long past a great many Samurai devoted themselves to the study of Jujutsu. However, unlike other types of martial arts, this training was kept hidden inside one's mind, spirit and body. Due to this, and the fact that unfortunately Jujutsu is not mentioned in history, there are no shortage of fellows spreading false rumors about this art.

柔術獨習法

其評を爲すの士少く又た曾て歴史上に於ても顯れざ
るなり之れ斯術の最も遺憾とする所ならぞや然と雖
も今や王政の世とは物變り文學盛に行はるゝにつれ
武道亦た再興の慮あり此時に膺りて尤も其必用を感
ずるものは柔術也撃劍之れに次ぎ弓馬槍術の如きは
其利用又稀れなり
夫れ柔術の今や世上に尊ばるゝ剛を制するが爲め而
已ならず屈せざるを挫く術ある而已ならず其裏必ず
犯すべからざる術あるを以てなり其術とは何ぞや曰
く死活自由の術なり

64

We live in a changing world under the rule of the Meiji Emperor (ruled 1867-1912,) where great advancements in learning are occurring. Despite this, my sole concern is the revitalization of marital arts training and though there are many martial arts, I feel Jujutsu is the best for this age since the chance to apply arts like Gekken (fencing with bamboo swords,) Yumi (the bow / archery,) Uma (horse/ equestrian arts) and Yari (spear) will be few and far between.

Jujutsu is of great benefit to the modern world. It is not used solely to control the strong and rigid but also can be applied to break the unyielding. It is ever vigilant against feints and surprise assaults. That is why it is known as Shikatsu Jiyu no Jutsu, techniques that can kill or revitalize as the user sees fit.

死活の術は柔術の奥秘にして之を試まんとする容易ならざるなり然りと雖も今日徳義地を拂ひ奸者横行の日に膺りては必ず柔剛を制するの術を知り兼て護身の楯となし又た扶弱挫強の術となすべし一言を書して之れを總論とす

四

The word Shikatsu refers to the resuscitation techniques that are part of the curriculum in Jujutsu schools. The same pressure points on the body that can be used to inflict maximum damage on an opponent can also be used to resuscitate victims. Jujutsu schools tend refer to these techniques as Inner Secrets and they are only taught to students who have attained a high level of training, due to their because of their difficulty.

Since the moral fabric is being swept away and villains wander the streets around us, knowledge of the techniques that allow the soft to control the rigid is essential. It becomes a defensive shield. To put it simply this book is about techniques that show how a seemingly weak challenger can topple a stronger opponent.

○柔術各流儀の事

柔術は古へより各々流儀のあるものにして其尤も流派の世に著しきものは揚心流、眞揚流、起倒流、神道流、及び一刀流、無雙流、の數派とす然して現今世人が聯習して容易たらしめ且つ其端緒を知ることを得るは無雙流起倒流の二派なり本書に於ては只々に或る流派の一部分を記し詳かに死活法の在點を判せしむるに足る著者の精神なれば三四法の流儀をして説明尤も細密確實ならしむる而已

Regarding the Different Jujutsu Schools

From days long past each school of Jujutsu had its own underlying philosophy. Some of the most well-known of the schools are:

揚心流 Yoshin School
真揚流 Shinnoke (Shinyo)School
起倒流 Kito School
神道流 Shindo School

In addition the Itto School and the Muso School are well known. These are some of the schools of martial arts modern practitioners can easily find and train in. However, the only two schools whose origins we can confirm are the Muso School and the Kito School.

The purpose of this book is to highlight just one part of one school and detail some of its techniques so the reader may gain a sense of what this Shikatsu Ho, Death-giving or Life-giving strategies are. It is the opinion of the author that by introducing 3 or 4 techniques from a school the underlying meaning will become apparent.

〇柔術形取勝敗の區別

以下數葉に於て柔術形取の方法を記載するに當り勝敗を判決するが爲め甲者乙者と區別をなし甲者をして活術を行ふべき勝者の一人となし乙者をして之れに對向する敗者の一人となす

本術は兩者相出會にして其一尺計りの距りを見て乙者甲者の胸襟を握り（握り方法乙四指を袖内にし親指を外にす）乙者尺計り引退く

How to Differentiate Between the Winner and Loser During Jujutsu Kata Training

On the following pages several examples of Jujutsu Kata-tori, or Kata training, will be detailed. In order to show who is the winner and who lost each bout, the combatants will be divided into Kosha and Otsusha. Koh and Otsu are common designations for ranking things and mean "former and latter." In Japanese they can be combined into one word Koh-Otsu to refer to two people in different roles, like in Jujutsu with an attacker and a defender. Adding the word "Sha" at the end means "the person who is" the former or latter. The illustration will indicate the Kohsha with the Kanji 甲 and the Otsusha with the Kanji 乙.

You, the Kohsha, will be the one executing the technique and therefore the winner of each bout. The Attacker, Otsusha, will be your opposite, trying to resist this technique and being defeated.

Technique #1 · Illustration 1

第　壹　圖

Koh
You

Otsu
Attacker

此際甲者は引いるゝまゝ第一圖に示するが如く腕に力を入れて止まる乙者此機を計り左手を以て甲者の左襟を摑み村雨（人体第一圖第十二及第三圖第六）項を見るべし即ち喉笛を締めんとす時早く、甲者第二圖の如く乙者の左手の

脈点（手腕屈伸筋）を親指にて摑み夫れと同時に左手を

Jujutsu Techniques #1 · Illustration 1

This technique begins with you and the Attacker approaching each other. When you are about 1 Shaku (30 cm) apart the attacker grabs the front of your shirt with his right hand. He should grip with four fingers inside the your collar and only his thumb on the outside.

The Attacker waits for an opening and draws back, trying to pull you with him. In response to this you fill your arms with power and resist the pull. This is shown in Illustration 1.

Technique #1 · Illustration 2

柔術獨習法

第二圖
甲乙

Koh
You

Otsu
Attacker

以て乙者の帯後へ手を廻し足を乙者の足と足との中間に入れ臀を押して第三圖の如く後へ倒し（自然に倒るゝに至るべし）（脈点は以前の如く摑み其屈伸を止め）然して手の尺澤（人躰第一圖第三十項を看るべし）即ち肘の處を押へ

左手にて乙者の村雨の處を締め再び第四圖の如く（襟を摑むと手を押へるを同時に事をなしうつむけとな

74

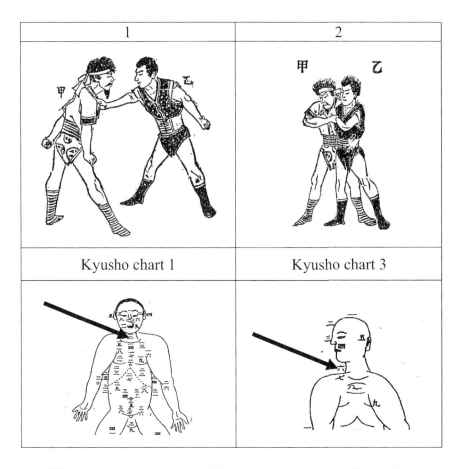

1	2
Kyusho chart 1	Kyusho chart 3

The Attacker has been waiting for this chance so he grabs your left collar with his left hand and attempts to choke you using the vital point Shigure. Shigure is the Nodo-bue, or windpipe and it is point #12 on Kyusho chart 1 and point #6 on Kyusho chart 3.

Note: It is not clear from the text or the illustration but my impression is the Attacker's right hand is gripping your right collar and his left hand is gripping your left collar. His hands are crossed and he pulling the two sides of your collar across your throat at the point called Shigure.

You respond by rapidly pressing into the vein on the Attacker's left arm with your thumb. This spot is on the tendon in the back of his left arm. At the same time wrap your left arm around the Attacker's back and place your foot between his feet.

Technique #1 · Illustrations 3 & 4

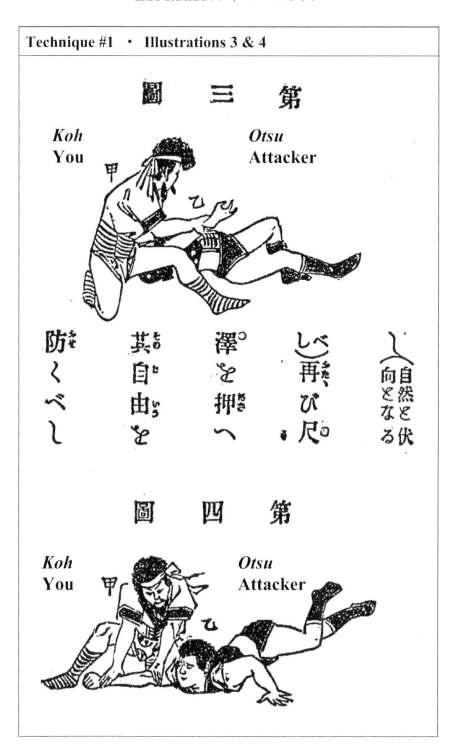

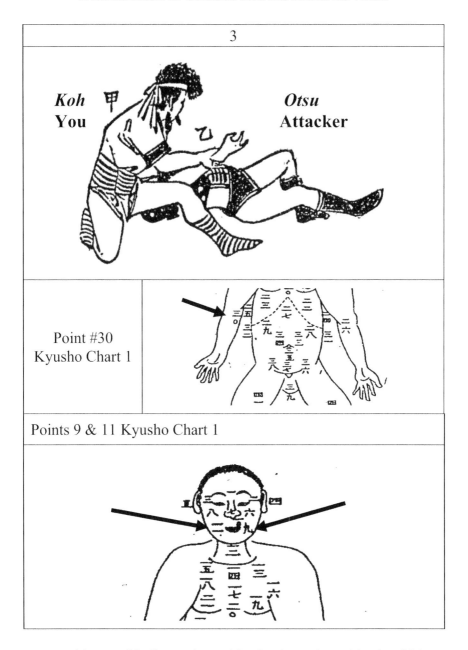

3

Koh　甲
You

Otsu
Attacker

Point #30
Kyusho Chart 1

Points 9 & 11 Kyusho Chart 1

　　Pushing on his liver, throw him backwards. This should be a natural movement to induce the fall and you should continue to push on the vein in the back of his arm to prevent it from bending.

　　Use the Kyusho called Sekizawa (See illustration)　In other words push the elbow down.

Finally, use your left hand to push on both sides of Shigure, Village Rain, the area under each cheekbone. These are Kyusho points 9 & 11.

Next, as shown in the fourth illustration, pull his collar and hand at the same time to bring him facedown. This should be a natural movement. Having done that once again push on Sekizawa in order to stop his movement.

Technique # 2 ・ Illustration 1

第　一　圖

Koh
You

Otsu
Attacker

甲

乙

〇全第二業（全上）

第一業と同じく両
者出會の業にして
乙者甲の胸襟を摑
むこと第一業の術
の如くなし村雨を
締めんとす時速か
に甲者は体を低く
なすと共に乙者の

Technique #2 Illustration 1

Koh
You

Otsu
Attacker

This technique starts the same as the previous one, with both combatants approaching each other. The attacker first grabs your right collar with his right hand. This is the same as in Technique #1. He then grabs your left collar with his left hand and attempts to choke you across Shigure.

Note:
This image is from Technique #4. It shows the two handed choke with the arms crossed.
This technique starts with you choking your opponent.

Technique # 2 ・ Illustration 2

体脇へ入り左手を以て

乙者の（摑みし手と手）村雨へ
（の中間へ入れ）

手を押入れ共に右手を

以て乙者の右足を摑み

上げ摑み處は（水月、人躰第
一圖第四十一

項を看るへし）水月を目ざすべし然して自然力を強め左手を以

て押すと同時片足を益々持上げ以て我が後へ倒伏す

べきの術なり

第　二　圖

Koh
You

Otsu
Attacker

甲

乙

二十

1	Point #41 Kyusho Chart 1

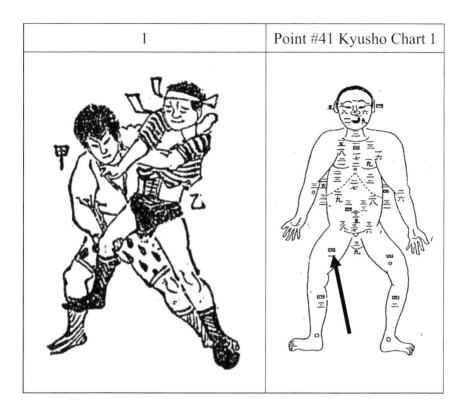

In response you should immediately drop your hips and reach under the attacker's crossed arms with your left arm to the point called Shigure, windpipe. Grip the attacker's windpipe with your left hand. As you grip and choke with your left hand, reach under the attacker's right thigh with your right hand and lift up. The point you seek to grab is called Suigetsu, moon reflected on water. This is point #41 in the diagram. Naturally* increase your strength pushing with your left hand as you pull up his right leg with your right hand. This technique allows you to throw the Attacker behind you.

*Note: By "naturally" the author probably means increase pressure in a smooth, steady manner.

Note: I was surprised that in this school Suigetsu was listed as being on the inside of the thigh. I have studied quite a few Kyusho charts from various traditional martial arts schools and Suigetsu has always been the solar plexus.

Technique # 3　・　Illustrations 1

第　壹　圖

Koh　　　　　　　　　*Otsu*
You　　　　　　　　**Attacker**

甲

乙

○全第三業

（全・上）

本業は途中通行の際
不慮の出來事にてし
則ち第一圖の如く甲
者後より抱き締む其
際乙者は之れを脱せ

Technique #3 · Illustration 1

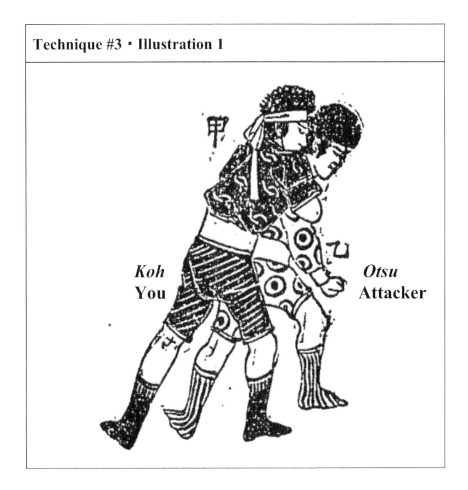

Koh
You

Otsu
Attacker

This technique is used when you are walking about and something unfortunate occurs.

Begin by reaching around and grabbing the Attacker from behind. The Attacker attempts to escape your grasp.

Note: I feel this technique is rather rare, a rear grab is usually an attack, but in this case it is used to subdue a ruffian.

Technique # 3 ・ Illustrations 2

んとするや、甲は直に
左手にて乙者の村雨
を押し右手は握拳を
揮て乙者の骨水（第二
看るへし）（腰骨の處
圖十七項を）を云ふ
（人躰）を力
のあらん限り押す之れと共に左足をして乙者の右
足をける則ち第二圖の有樣にして我目前へ倒すべし
（既に倒る〻や氣絶せり研者は
習聯中篤く注意をなすへし）

第 二 圖

Koh
You

Otsu
Attacker

2	Point #17 Kyusho Chart 2
Koh *Otsu* You Attacker	

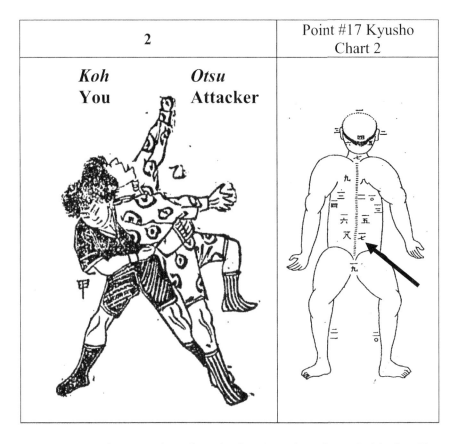

You reach around and grab the Attacker from behind. The Attacker attempts to escape your grasp. Use your left hand to apply pressure to Shigure, the windpipe, and make a fist with your right hand. Plant your fist on the point known as Kotsu Sui, just to the right of the spine just above the hip bone, and push. This point is shown in Kyusho Chart 2 Point #17.

Push on Kotsu Sui as hard as you can and, at the same time. Kick the Attacker's right foot out with your left foot. This is shown in the second illustration. This should cause the attacker to fall down in front of you.

You should exercise caution when doing this technique with training partners as they may hurt themselves when falling or they may pass out.

Technique # 4 ・ Illustrations 1

（既に倒るゝや氣絶せり研者は
習聯中篤く注意をなすべし）

足をける則ち第二圖の有様にして我目前へ倒すべ

のあらん限きり押すぞれと共に左足をして乙者の右

○全第四業（全上）

第四業は以前の反對に

して其執業は尤も面白

くして且つ妙なり則ち

第一圖に示する如く最

初甲者乙者の両襟を双手にて摑む乙者亦た屈せずし

て甲の双襟を摑まんとするや其業に先きだち第二圖

第　壹　圖

乙

甲

Koh
You

Otsu
Attacker

Technique #4

The technique in #4 is the opposite of technique #3 and starts with you taking the opponent's collar from the front. The way this technique unfolds is very interesting and subtle.

This technique starts, as shown in the illustration, with you grabbing the lapels of the Attacker's shirt with both hands. Your left hand on his right lapel and your left hand on his right. He immediately responds by grabbing both of your lapels in the same fashion.

Technique # 4 · Illustrations 2 & 3

柔術獨習法

本業は第一圖の如く甲者座

○第五業　（仝上）

行ふべし

再び第一業の第三圖の術を

者の双襟を締め而して後ち

Koh
You

Otsu
Attacker

第二圖

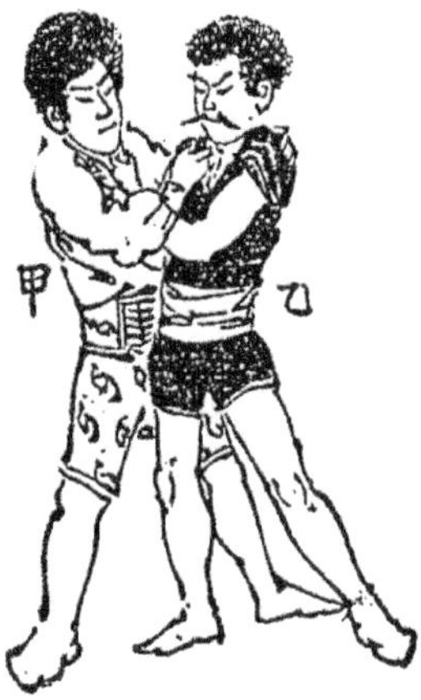

の如く左手を乙者の左
肩へ廻し足を圖の如く
にし、我後へ倒すべし（此
双自然に倒る）而して倒る
や否や第三圖の如く乙

第三圖

Koh
You

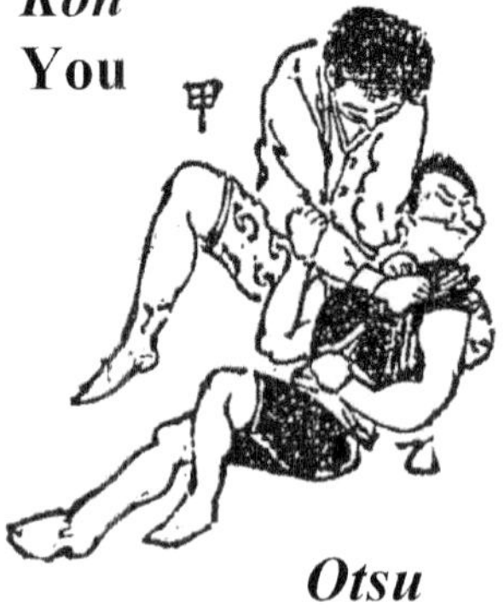

甲

乙

Otsu
Attacker

Then, as the second illustration shows, wrap your left arm behind the Attacker and grab his left shoulder. Place your legs as shown in the second illustration. Next, topple the opponent backwards, this should be done in a natural manner. The moment you have your Attacker on the ground grab both lapels and choke, as shown in illustration 3. Finish the technique as shown in illustrations 3 & 4 of technique #1.

Technique # 5 ・ Illustrations 1

○第五業　（仝上）

本業は第一圖の如く甲者座

第　壹　圖

甲　　乙

Koh
You

Otsu
Attacker

二十四

乙者は甲の尺斗り

の距りを以て右手を

摑み、我許へ引寄せる

（摑み處は脈處にして

手腕屈伸筋を指す）時早く

も甲は踵を開くと共に

乙の摑まんとすべ

き右手を第二圖の如

く摑み夫れと同時に

体を乙者の胸許へ入

れ甲右手を以て乙の

Technique #5

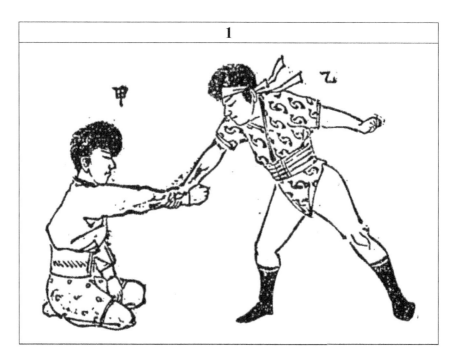

This technique begins with you seated as shown in illustration one. The Attacker walks towards you, and when he has judged the best distance, grabs your right arm and attempts to pull you forward. The grab should put pressure on the tendon in the back of the arm.

Technique # 5　・　Illustrations 2

左足を取り体を委ねて
我が右肩上より後へ逆
投せしむべき妙術也

（解）
甲者〳〵の如く頭より
休を自然に乙の腕許
へ入る（共に甲者右足は影
線の如く延すべし）

〇第六業　（全上）
柔術は本第六業を以て
業を終へ以下劔術の部に轉るべし

第　貳　圖

Koh　　　*Otsu*
You　　**Attacker**

The Attacker tries to add his left hand to griping your right arm. In response you immediately shoot your heel out and rip your right arm free. Grab the Attacker's left arm with your left hand. This is shown in illustration 2.

At the same time thrust your body towards the Attacker's Mune-moto, base of his chest. Use your right hand to grab the Attacker's left leg. The rest you leave up to your body. Bring your right shoulder up, flip the attacker over and behind you. This is a very subtle and mysterious technique.

Additional Explanation: Your head should follow the dotted line to naturally meet the Attacker's Mune-moto. You should also note the outline which shows the right leg extending.

Technique #6 · Illustration 1

○第六業 （全上）

柔術は本第六業を以て

業を終へ以下劔術の部に轉るべし

第 一 圖

甲

乙

Koh
You

Otsu
Attacker

二十六

因に記す柔術は本

書に於ても各流派

に則ち記載すべき

本意なれども余は

先きに傳圖解雄応と題

し世に公頒したれ

ば足らさる處該書

に就て看らるべし

故に本書は生に死

活灸所を記すに足

96

Technique #6

This technique begins with you seated and armed with a Tanken, short sword. The Attacker is facing you with a Choken, long sword. The Attacker begins to advance on you so respond by cutting to his face with your Tanken. The Attacker immediately blocks this cut with his Choken.

Note: Typically Japanese swords are called Daito and Shoto, for the long and short sword. In this case the swords seem to be western style sabers, which were the ones carried by Japanese Police Officers in this era.

Technique #6 ・ Illustration 2

柔術獨習法

而已看者之れを諒せよ

本業は甲者短劍を以て座し乙者長劍を以て向ふも

第一圖の如く短劍を揮て乙者の面に對して切込む時乙者は直に長劍をして其儘受止むるや

否や乙者左手をして甲者の右

手（短劔を持ちし）を摑み（灸所を摑むへし）共に

長劍を捨て甲者の胸襟に對向す則ち第二圖の如くなし時甲

者短劍を捨て左手をして第三圖に示せる如く其体格

第 二 圖

Koh
You

Otsu
Attacker

98

The moment he blocks your cut, the Attacker grabs your right forearm with his right hand. So he has seized the hand you are holding your short sword with and he is pressing on a Kyusho, vital point. He then drops his longsword and grabs your left collar in his left hand. This is shown in illustration 2.

Technique #6 · Illustration 3

柔 術 獨 習 法

Koh　　　　*Otsu*
You　　　　Attacker

圖　參　第

秘訣圖解
柔術獨習法大尾

の体裁をも構込み甲者右足を以て乙の左足に掛け右

手をして帶間を抑すと左手を我許へ引くと之の三業を

一括し技術最も敏捷に扱ひ

我躰を捨て則ち乙者の力を

借りて我頭上より逆投せし

むべし柔にして剛を制防す

べきの術此等にある哉

二十八

Koh
You

Otsu
Attacker

Next, as shown in illustration 3, drop your short sword and move your body as shown. Hook your right leg around the Attacker's right leg and with your right hand push on the center of his Obi, or belt. Finally, pull with your left hand, which is gripping his left wrist. Using these three points of contact deftly and in unison, throw your body away by falling back and using the Attacker's body weight to throw him backwards over your head. Truly using a soft, flexible method to overthrow a strong but rigid attacker is what this technique is all about.

End

Secret Illustrated Guide to Solo Jujutsu Training

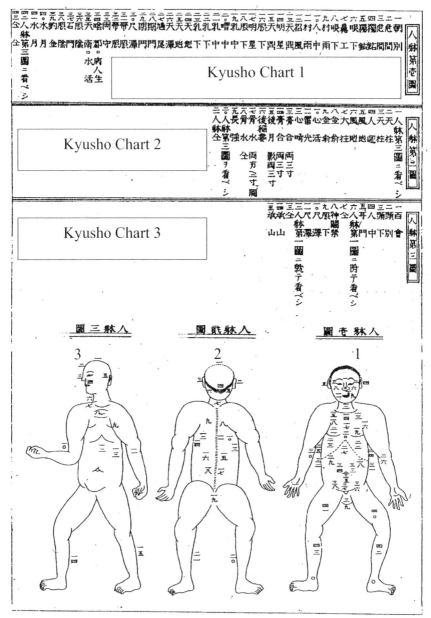

Note: This is the most ridiculous format for a Kyusho chart. The text is minuscule, the numbering is complex and overlapping and there are several inconsistencies.

兵法要務∴

柔術剣棒図解秘訣

Excerpt from:

Heihoyomu:
Jujutsu Kenbo Zukai
Hiketsu

**Fundamentals of
Military Strategy:
An Illustrated
Guide to the Secrets
of Jujutsu, Kenjutsu
and Bojutsu**

井口松之助
By
Inoguchi
Matsunosuke

Published
1887

Cover of *Fundamentals of Military Strategy*

Translator's introduction

I've been interested in translating *Jujutsu Kenbo Zukai Hiketsu Fundamentals of Military Strategy* for a long time, however the complexity of the language was a barrier. Japan dramatically simplified the official writing style post World War 2, so any books before that are quite complex. In addition, this is the earliest post-Meiji Restoration illustrated guide to martial arts that I have found. In the years following the release of this book, dozens of other authors followed suit and published illustrated guides to various martial arts. The success of this book may have been the catalyst that started a whole new genre. Though there is little information about the life of Inoguchi, he authored several books about martial arts. This makes it likely he was from a Samurai family that served as martial arts instructors for one of the former domains of Japan. This book was an attempt to make the transition from an employee of the government to a citizen earning a living selling martial arts instruction.

While this book also covers sword and wooden staff fighting techniques in addition to passages on military strategy and mental preparation, only the Jujutsu techniques from the Tenjin Shinyō-ryū Jujutsu school will be included in this volume. In addition, due to the length, complexity and difficulty of the Japanese in this book only the first two sections, Tehodoki and Shodan of Jujutsu will be translated. I hope to include the next two sections in future volumes and the whole book at some point in the near future.

Overall the edition of this book is in poor condition, but I have done my best to clean up each pages and I had to consult several editions of this book in order to make a complete set.

Issues with translation

From 1887 to 1895 *Fundamentals of Military Strategy* went through over a dozen printings, each time adding and correcting some sections. I actually used a combination of three editions due to some missing pages. The author alternates between a person's right or left and the viewer's right or left which can be quite confusing. I have done my best to visualize these techniques and correct all such instances to the person's right and left, not the viewers. The biggest issue was in the description of the techniques. Transitions from one movement to the next were rather unclear in some cases. To solve this I consulted two other books associated with this school. These sources were published in the years after *Fundamentals of Military Strategy*. They are *Illustrated Guide to the Inner Mysteries of Tenjin Shinyo School Jujutsu* (1893) and *Tenshin School Jujutsu* (1926.) Both books contain the same list of techniques from *Fundamentals of Military Strategy*, therefore, for clarity, I combined the explanations from the three books into each technique.

- The names of the Kata have been translated into English but these are approximate.
- The Kiai/Kake-goe sounds are quite varied
- There are many symbols used to indicate where one sentence ends and the other begins.
- I included images from the 1893 and the 1926 versions when the illustrations were helpful by showing a different angle or different portion of the technique.
- As the before and after illustrations show, some of the pages needed to be digitally cleaned.

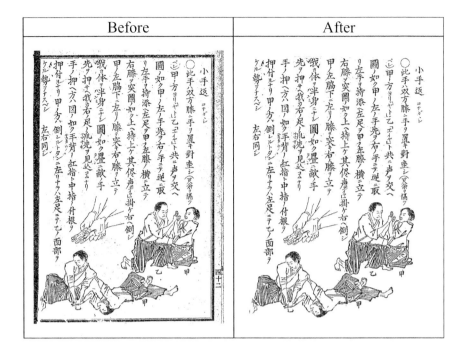

The primary source is:

- **兵法要務：柔術剣棒図解秘訣**
  Heihoyomu: Jujutsu Kenbo Zukai Hiketsu
  Fundamentals of Military Strategy:
  An Illustrated Guide to the Secrets of Jujutsu, Kenjutsu and Bojutsu
  By Inoguchi Matsunosuke 井口松之助. Published 1887.

I also compared the techniques listed in this book with the following two similar books. I included some images from these books when it seemed helpful in fleshing out what happens in a given technique.

● 天神真楊流柔術極意教授図解

Tenjin Shinyo Ryu Jujutsu Gokui Kyoju Zukai Jujutsu

Illustrated Guide to the Inner Mysteries of Tenjin Shinyo School Jujutsu

By Yoshida Chiharu 吉田千春 and Iso Mataemon 磯又右衛門

Published 1893

This is a curious book since it basically remakes Kenbo Zukai with more Jujutsu techniques, but uses different and strangely briefer descriptions of the techniques along with new illustrations. It will be referred to as the "1893 Version."

● 天神鉄真流柔術型極意秘伝図解：報国館鉄仲流

Tenjin Tesshin Ryu Jujutsu Kata Gokui Hiden Zukai: Hokoku Kan Tecchu Ryu

Illustrated Guide to the Inner Secrets of Tenshin School Jujutsu Kata: Hokoku Hall Tecchu School

By Kushi Niju 大串仁十

Published 1926

It will be referred to as the "1926 Version."

This illustration starts the section on Jujutsu. It shows what the inside of Dojo looked in the Meiji Era and probably reflects how Jujutsu training was done in previous Edo Era. The Sensei is seated up on a raised platform. The calligraphy above him reads 柔制剛 *The soft and flexible can topple the strong and rigid.*

柔術ハ古クヨリ其妙ヲ傳ヘ治亂ニ亘リ學ハサル可カラ
サルノ要術ナリ其術タル所謂柔能ク剛ヲ制スルノ道ニ
シテ我ニ勝レルカ者ト雖ヒ容易ク之ヲ捕挫ギ已ヲ全フ
シテ必勝ヲ保ツノ術ナリ夫カハ限アリ術ハ限リナシ謂
ハンヤ死活ヲ自在ニシ其奧ヲ極ムルニ至ッテハ夭死者
メ克ク蘇活セシムルアリ嗚呼該世ノ衆實ニ學バス
有ル可カラズ其流派ノ世ニ著キモノハ揚心流神道流
揚流起倒流寺ナリ流義ニ因リ教法大同小異アリト雖

其奧妙ニ至ッテハ一ナリ

The Origin and Significance of Jujutsu

From days of old Samurai have trained in Jujutsu. Whether in peacetime or in war it was considered a fundamental art. What I am describing is the art where the soft and flexible conquers the strong and rigid. Even if you are facing an opponent who is much stronger, you can easily seize and break them. Jujutsu is an art that allows you to consistently achieve victory because,

There is a limit to strength but technique has no limits.

Jujutsu grants you the power to take life or give it. If you become enlightened to the Okugi, inner mysteries, of Jujutsu then you will be able to both topple your enemies and revive those that have been attacked or had an accident. Thus I beseech the average citizen to study the art of Jujutsu. Some of the more renowned schools are the Yoshin School, the Shinto School, the Tenshin Shinyo School and the Kito School. The way these schools teach Jujutsu is largely the same, varying only in the details, however the inner meaning is the same.

一柔術ハ受方ヲ甲者ト為シ捕方ヲ乙者ト為ス手術表裏
ノ解書ノ盡サ丶ルハ圖画ヲ以テ辨シ圖画ノ及ハサル
ハ又書ニ讓ル讀者茅一圖ヨリ第二圖第三圖ト係連シ
テ視ルベシ仕組手解抬二組初段居捕立合都合二拾組
投捨二拾組口傳秘決多シト雖モ大緊ネ之ヲ洩ス事ナ
シ其書画ニ盡シ難キ物ハ目録ノミヲ挙テ粗畧スル所
アリ

How to Use This Book

The person receiving the technique in Jujutsu is the Uke Kata "receiver" and the person doing the technique is the Tori Kata "engager." In this volume the receiver will be called Kosha, or Former, and the engager will be the Otsusha, or Latter.

In order to make this volume of Shujutsu, Hand Techniques, easily understandable I have included illustrations along with the explanations. If questions remain after examining the illustrations please refer back to the text. The reader should follow the progression of the techniques from illustration 1, to illustration 2 and on to illustration 3.

Note: To ease understanding the person doing the technique will be "you" and the person receiving will be "the Attacker."

柔術ノ部

手解　十二手
鬼拳、振解、逆手、逆指、片胸捕、兩胸捕
小手返、兩手捕、氣捕、天倒、扱捕、打手

初段居捕　十手
眞之位、添捕、御前捕、袖車、飛違、拔身目附、
鎧返、兩手捕、壁添、後捕

初段立合　十手
行違、突掛、引落、兩胸捕、連拍子、友車、衣被、襟投、手髪捕、後捕

投捨　二十手
鐘木、刈捨、朽木倒、腰車、横車、片胸捕、手髪捕、小具足、腰刈捨、獨鈷
小手返、引落、手繰、捨身、下り藤、腕絡、矢筈、兩手捕、兩挊捕、後捕

乱捕　二十手
構捕、小手シギ、襟捕、突込、胴〆、組合突込、捨身、腕シギ、肌我、
腰投、捨身投、背負投

The techniques translated in this volume: 22

Total Jujutsu techniques in this book: 72

Jujutsu Techniques
- 12 *Shikumi Tehodoki*, or Freeing Seized Hands techniques.
- 10 *Shodan Idori,* or First Level Responding to a Sanding Attack techniques.
- 10 *Shodan Tachi-ai,* or First Level Responding to Armed and Unarmed Attacks
- 20 *Shodan Nagesute,* or First Level Sacrifice Throw techniques.
- 20 Randori, Free Sparring techniques

There are many Kuden, oral transmissions, and Hiketsu, deep secrets, in these techniques so, illustrations can't do them justice. Therefore only the Mokuroku level of Jujutsu training is listed.

Note: The rank of Mokuroku

A Mokuroku is a list or catalog that indicates a practitioner has achieved a certain level of proficiently, therefore it could be considered "a letter of rank." The reason it is a "list" or "catalogue" is because it only contains the names of a section of techniques. The document itself is fairly simple, it typically has the name of the school, the word Mokuroku at the beginning, the list of techniques in the center and ends with official signatures and stamps. There may be a list of all the heads of the school in chronological order until the current head.

Tehodoki: Freeing Your Hands
12 Techniques

1. 鬼拳 Onigoshi/ Oni Kobushi: Devil's Fist
2. 振解 Furi-hotoki: Shake Free
3. 逆手 Gyaku Te: Reverse Grip
4. 逆指 Gyaku Yubi: Bending the Fingers Back
5. 片胸捕 Kata Mune Dori: Defense Against One Handed Chest Grab
6. 両胸捕 Ryomune Dori: Defense Against a Two-Handed Chest Grab
7. 小手返 Kote Gaeshi: Bending Back the Hand
8. 両手返 Ryote Kaeshi: Two-Handed Reverse
9. 気捕 Kidori: Seizing the Chance
10. 天倒 Tento: Top of the Head
11. 扱捕 Mogi Dori: Plucking Away
12. 打手 Uchi Te: Striking Hand

Shodan Idori
10 Techniques

1. 真之位 Shin no Kurai: True Stance
2. 添捕 Soe-dori: Alongside Seizure
3. 御前捕 Gozen Dori: Before Royalty Technique
4. 袖車 Sode Guruma: Sleeve Wheel
5. 飛違 Tobi Chigai: Leaping In and Attacking (Reversing the Situation)
6. 抜身目付 Nukimi Metsuke: Locking Eyes and Drawing
7. 鐺返 Kojiri Gaeshi: Reversing the Scabbard Cap
8. 両手捕 Ryo-te Dori: Responding to a Two-Handed Attack
9. 壁添 Kabe Soi: Pressed Against a Wall
10. 後捕 Ushiro Dori: Responding when Attacked from Behind

手解 Tehodoki: Freeing Your Hands
鬼拳 Onigoshi: Devil's Fist 1/12

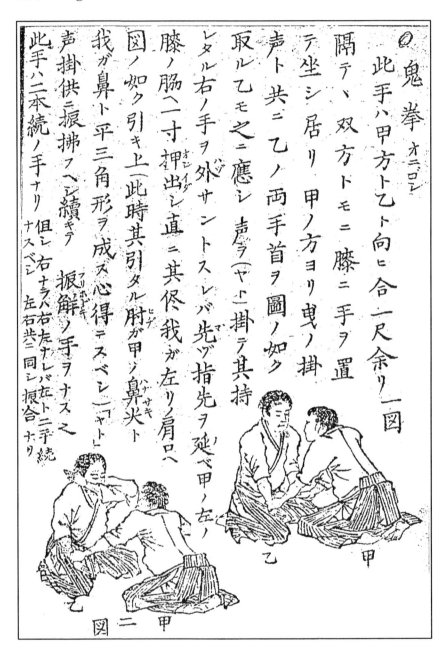

此手ハ二本續ノ手ナリ但シ右ナラハ右左ナレバ左ト二手續
聲掛供ニ振拂ヘシ續キテ　ナスベシ左右共ニ同シ振合ナリ
我ガ鼻ト平三角形ヲ成ス心得テスベレ）「ヤト」振解ノ手ヲ　ナスヘシ
圖ノ如ク引キ上（此時其引タル肘ガ甲ノ鼻火ト
膝ノ脇ヘ二寸押出シ直ニ其侭我ガ左リ肩ロヘ
レタル右ノ手ヲ外サントスレバ先ヅ指先ヲ延ベ甲ノ左ノ
取ル乙モ之ニ應シ聲ヲ（ヤ）掛テ其持
聲ト共ニ乙ノ兩手首ヲ圖ノ如ク
テ坐シ居リ甲ノ方ヨリ乙ノ手ヲ掛
隔テ、双方トモニ膝ニ手ヲ置
此手ハ甲方ト乙ト向ヒ合一尺余リ一圖

○鬼拳　オニコレ

手解 Tehodoki: Freeing Your Hands
鬼拳 Onigoshi: Devil's Fist

For this technique you and the Attacker are seated in Seiza, with your hands on your knees, facing each other in Seiza about 1 Shaku, 30 centimeters, apart.

The Attacker shouts a Kakegoe of *Ei!* (The author uses the Kanji 曳 "to pull" for this sound) He grabs both your wrists. This is shown in illustration 1. To free your left hand use a Kakegoe of *Yato!* and strongly flex the tips of your fingers. Push your left hand slightly towards the side of the Attacker's left knee. Then immediately yank your hand up as hard as you can over your right shoulder as shown in illustration 2.

The ideal way to do this technique is to end up with your elbow level with the Attacker's nose. His nose, your nose and your elbow should form the three points of a triangle. You should use a Kakegoe of *Ya!* as you Furi-harau, shake off and sweep away, the hand gripping your wrist. After finishing this technique you should move on to the next technique Furi Hodoki. This is the second technique in the Shodan level.

Since it is best to do the technique on both sides, after doing the left hand, you should do the right hand. The right side is considered to be the second part of this technique. Both sides are done in the same manner.

Note: The use of left and right is very inconsistent in this description and has been adjusted to match the illustrations.

手解 Tehodoki: Freeing Your Hands 2/12
振解 Furi-hotoki: Shake Free

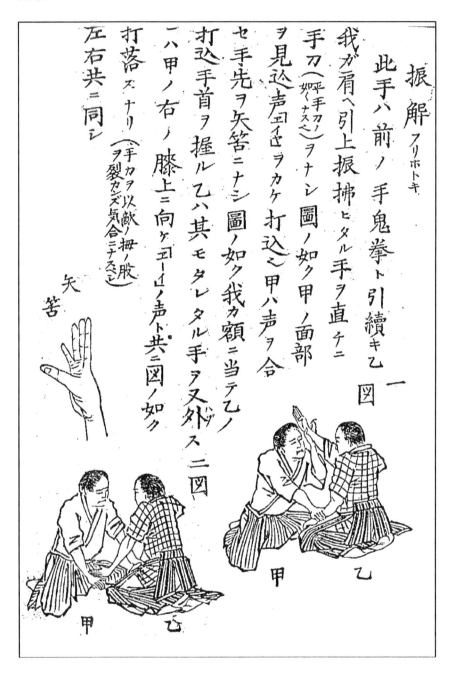

振解 フリホトキ

此手ハ前ノ手鬼拳ト引續キ乙図

我ガ肩ヘ引上振拂ヒタル手ヲ直ニ一

手刀（鯉手刀ニナス）ヲナシ図ノ如ク甲ノ面部

ヲ見込声ヲイサヲカケ打込ニ甲ハ声ヲ合

セ手先ヲ矢筈ニナシ　図ノ如ク我ガ額ニ当テ乙ノ

打込手首ヲ握ル乙ハ其モタレタル手ヲ又外ス二図

一ハ甲ノ右ノ膝上ニ向ヶヨーイ山ノ声ト共ニ図ノ如ク

打落スナリ（手刀ヲ以敵ノ拇ノ股ヲ裂カンズ気合ニナスシ）

左右共ニ同シ

矢
筈

甲

乙

甲
乙

手解 Tehodoki: Freeing Your Hands
振解 Furi-hotoki: Shake free

This technique is a continuation of the previous technique, Devil's Fist.

1	2	Yahazu

Strike down to Men (top of the head) with the right hand you yanked free using Devil's Fist. Your hand should be in a Shuto, or Hand Sword. This is also known as Hira Shuto, or Flat Hand Sword.

Note: The Kanji for this could also be read as Te-Gatana.

As the illustration shows, you pick your target on the Attacker's head and with a Kakegoe of *Ei-ya!* strike the Attacker in the head. The Attacker matches your Kiai with one of his own and catches your wrist. He has his hand shaped like a Yahazu, the nock of an arrow. See the separate illustration of how this is done.

To free your right hand from the Attacker's grip, use a cry of *Eih!* and cut your hand downward, toward the Attacker's right knee. This is shown in illustration 2.

The left and right sides are done the same way. When attacking with the Shuto, envision yourself striking down with enough power to snap the bone at the base of the thumb.

Note: Illustration 1 shows how the technique begins with the right hand, however illustration 2 shows the final position with the left hand.

手解 Tehodoki: Freeing Your Hands 3/12
逆手 Gyaku Te: Reverse Grip

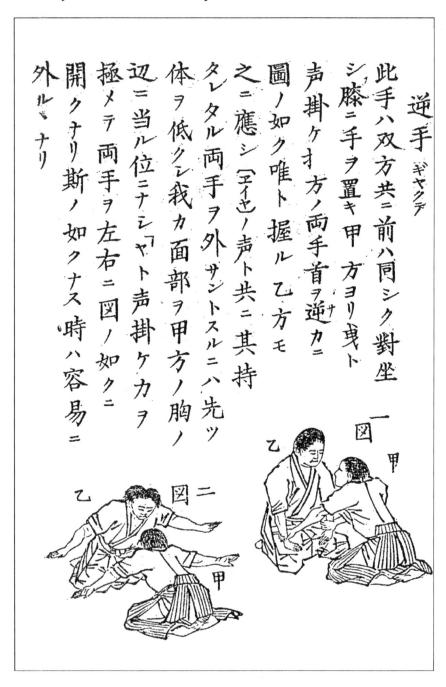

逆手 ギヤクテ

此手ハ双方共ニ前ハ同シク對坐

シ膝ニ手ヲ置キ甲方ヨリ曳ト

声掛ケオカノ両手首ヲ逆カニ

圖ノ如ク唯ト握ル乙方モ

之ニ應シ〔ヱイヤ〕ノ声ト共ニ其持

タレタル両手ヲ外サントスルニハ先ツ

体ヲ低クレ我カ面部ヲ甲方ノ胸ノ

辺ニ当ル位ニナレヤト声掛ケカヲ

挫メテ両手ヲ左右ニ図ノ如クニ

開クナリ斯ノ如クナス時ハ容易ニ

外ルヽナリ

逆手 Gyaku Te: Reverse Grip

This technique uses both hands. It is similar to the previous two techniques since you and the Attacker are seated facing each other with your hands on your knees.

1	2
乙 Otsu　　甲 Koh You　　　Attacker	乙 Otsu　　甲 Koh You　　　Attacker

The attacker does a Kakegoe of *Ei!* and grabs both your hands in a reverse grip, as shown in illustration 1, with your thumbs down and your palms facing outward. In response to this you should do the following; with a Kakegoe of *Ei-ya!* push your face towards the Attacker's chest, thereby lowering your body. Your head should nearly strike him in the chest. Next, with a Kakegoe of *Yato!* whip both arm out to the side as shown in illustration 2.

手解 Tehodoki: Freeing Your Hands 4/12
逆指 Gyaku Yubi: Bending the Fingers Back

逆指

此手ハ前ニ同シク双方對坐
シ膝ニ手ヲオキ甲方ヨリ
〔ヤ〕ト声掛ケ共ニ乙ノ手先
ヲ握リ指ヲメシ上ケントス
乙カ方ハ之レニ應シ声ヲ掛ケ
我カ肘ヲ腰脇ニ當テ拇指ヲ
屈メテ挿図ノ如ク取止メテメサセ
ヌナリ

逆指 Gyaku Yubi: Bending the Fingers Back

This technique starts out the same as the previous technique. You and the Attacker are sitting facing each other with your hands on your knees.

With a Kake-goe of *Ya!* the attacker grabs your fingers, squeezes and tries to raise them up. Respond with a Kake-goe of your own and press your elbows into your sides, squeezing your armpits tight. Bend in the thumb of your left hand towards your palm and squeeze. This is shown in the detail illustration. This will stop the attacker from being able to bend your fingers up.

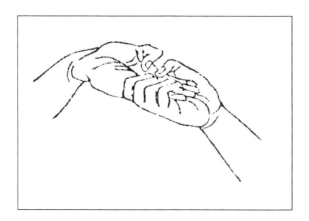

手解 Tehodoki: Freeing Your Hands 5/12
片胸捕 Kata Mune Dori: Defense Against One Handed Chest Grab

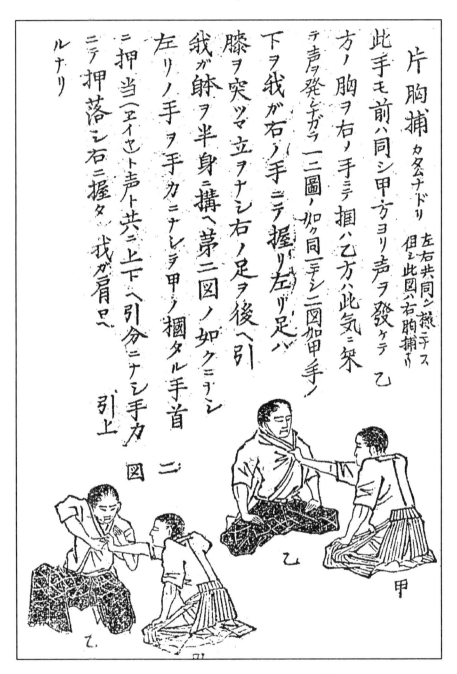

片胸捕 Kata Mune Dori: Defense Against One Handed Chest Grab

This technique is the same on both the left and right sides, however the illustrations show only the right side. This technique starts out the same as the previous one.

The Attacker shouts a Kake-goe and grabs your collar with his right hand. You use this attack to gather your strength and shout a Kake-goe in response. Then do as shown in illustrations 1 & 2. With your right hand grab your shirt just below where the Attacker grabbed you. Put your weight on your left knee and pull your right leg back. This will cause your body to open up to one side. You are now perpendicular in relation to the Attacker.

Form your left hand into a Shuto, Hand Sword, and with a Kake-goe of *Eiya!* strike the wrist of the Attacker's right hand, which is holding your shirt. You are simultaneously striking from above with your left hand and pulling with your right hand from below. Your right hand should pull up towards your right shoulder.

手解 Tehodoki: Freeing Your Hands 6/12
両胸捕 Ryomune Dori:
Defense Against a Two-Handed Chest Grab

両胸捕 リャウムナトリ 此図ハ右両胸捕ノ図ナリ

○此手モ前ハ同ヤウナリ 甲ノ方ヨリ声ヲ

ヤ上掛ケ乙ノ胸襟ヲ双手ニテ取ル乙ハ掛

声ニ答ヘ我ガ腰ヲ少シク延べ所謂中ゴシ

（甲ノ右ノ手ヲ上ニ有ヒハ右両胸捕ト号シテ左

ノ手ヲ上ニ有ヒハ左ノ両胸捕ト号ス）圖ノ如ク今我ガ

左ノ手ト右ノ膝ヲ立左リヲ膝突ツマ立ルナリ甲方ノ

両手ノ上ニ押当（ヤ上ト掛声ト共ニ少シ腰ヲ下ル途端ニ甲ノ両手

ノスキガアク故図ノ如ク我ガ左ノ手先ヲ差入揷画ノ如ク我ガ右ノ

手ニテ握リ（ヤ上）声ト共ニ下ヨリコジ上ルナリ（又解甲ノ左ノ）其途手ヲ解ルナリ

端ニ左右ノ足ヲ立替右ノ足膝突左リ足ヲ立膝ヲナシテ残リ

タル甲ノ右ニテ捫タル手ヲ前ノ片胸捕ノ如ニ打拂フベレ左右共同ジ

両胸捕 Ryomune Dori:
Defense Against a Two-Handed Chest Grab

This illustration shows the technique Defense Against a Two-Handed Chest Grab on the right. This technique begins from the same position as the previous one.

The Attacker shouts a Kake-goe of *Yaa!* and grabs your left and right collar at chest level with both hands. Respond with your own Kake-goe and raise your hips up off the ground. Raising your hips up off the ground like this is known as Naka-goshi, literally "middle hips." If the attacker's right hand is on top then the technique is called Migi Ryomune Dori, Right Defense Against a Two-Handed Chest Grab, if his left hand is on top then it is called Hidari Ryomune Dori, Left Defense Against a Two-Handed Chest Grab.

As the illustration shows, you should next put your weight on your left knee and stand up on your right foot as you raise your left hand. Push down on the top of the Attacker's arms with your left hand. Shout a Kake-goe of *Yaa!* and, at the same time, drop your hips slightly.

The moment you do this a gap will open up between the Attacker's arms. As the illustration shows, make use of this chance and slip your arm in between the opponent's and clasp your hands together.

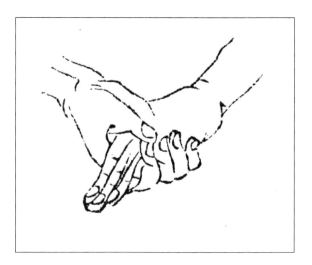

Join your left hand to your right as shown in the detail illustration. With a Kake-goe of *Yato!* bring your hips up. This will cause the Attacker's left hand to release. From there immediately switch your feet by dropping your right knee to the ground and standing up on your left foot. Knock off the Attacker's remaining hand by striking with a Shuto in the same way as described in Kata Mune Dori. The left and right sides are done the same way.

The illustration from the 1893 edition shows the overall positioning much clearer.

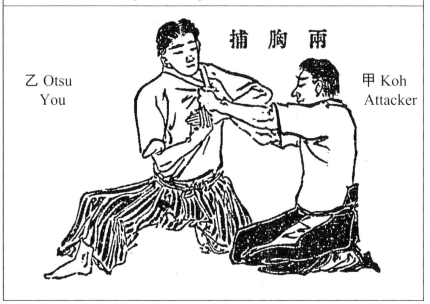

乙 Otsu
You

兩 胸 捕

甲 Koh
Attacker

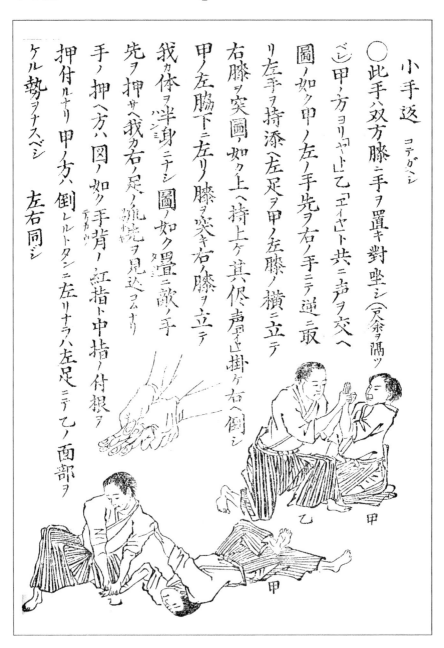

（小手返）コテガヘシ

○此手ハ双方膝ニ手ヲ置キ對坐シ（尻ヲ隔ツ

ベシ）甲ノ方ヨリ「ヤッ」ト乙「エイ」サト共ニ声ヲ交ヘ

圖ノ如ク甲ノ左ノ手先ヲ甲ノ左膝ノ横ニ立テ右ノ手ニテ逆ニ取

リ左ノ手ヲ持添ヘ左足ヲ甲ノ右ノ手ヲ右ノ膝ノ横ニ立テ

右膝ヲ突圖ノ如ク上ヘ持上ゲ其儘声ヲ掛ケ右ヘ倒シ

甲ノ左脇下ニ左リ膝ヲ突キ右ノ膝ヲ立テ

我カ体ヲ半身ニナシ圖ノ如ク疊ニ敷ノ手

先ヲ押サヘ我カ右ノ足ノ焼キヲ見込ムナリ

手ノ押ヘ方ハ圖ノ如ク手背ノ紅指ト中指ノ付根ヲ

押付ルナリ甲ノ方ハ倒レルトタンニ左足ニテ乙ノ面部ヲ

ケル勢ルナスベシ　左右同シ

小手返 Kote Gaeshi: Bending Back the Hand

This technique begins with you and the Attacker facing each other seated in Seiza, traditional Japanese sitting style. Both combatants should have their hands on their knees. You should be about 1 Shaku, 30 centimeters, apart.

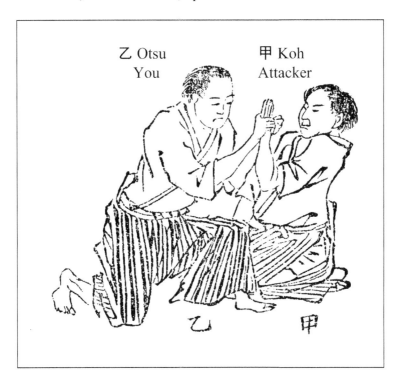

As soon as the Attacker begins a Kake-goe of *Yato!* you should respond with your own Kake-goe of *Eiya!* Then grab the end of the Attacker's left hand with your right hand and twist the wrist around.

This is called Gyaku ni Tori, "Taking a Reverse." Join your left hand beside your right hand and plant your left foot beside the Attacker's left knee. Keep your weight on your right knee as shown in the illustration. After brining the Attacker's hand up, do a Kake-goe of *Eiya!* and topple the opponent to your right. End with your left knee planted below the Attacker's left armpit.

乙 Otsu   甲 Koh
You   Attacker

Turn your right knee upright so your body is twisted Han-mi, or perpendicular to the Attacker. As shown in the illustration you have forced the tips of the Attacker's fingers into the Tatami mat. You should be facing the direction the toes of your right foot point, as if you are staring at them.

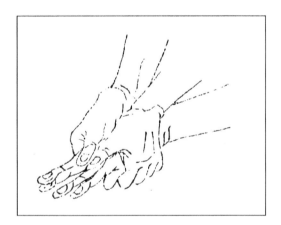

The detail illustration shows how to take the Gyaku. It is important to note that you are pushing on the base of the middle fingers and ring finger with your thumbs. The moment the Attacker is toppled over he should attempt a strong kick at your face. If he has toppled on his left side, then kick with your left foot. The left and right sides are done the same way.

Illustrations 1 & 2 from the 1893 edition

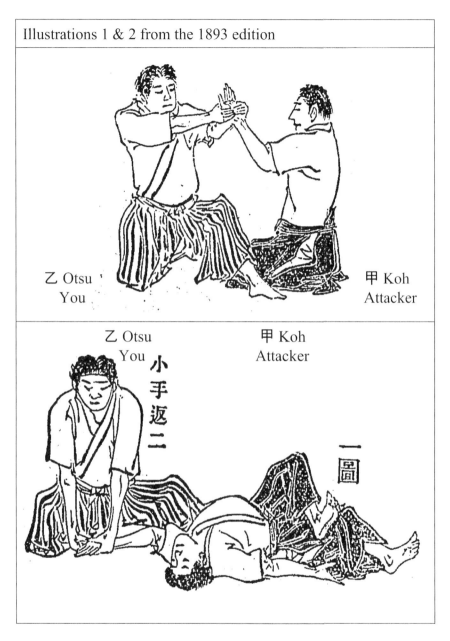

乙 Otsu
You

甲 Koh
Attacker

乙 Otsu
You

甲 Koh
Attacker

小手返二

一圖

Note: The Kote Gaeshi from the 1893 edition has some interesting differences. The left foot is on the ground and the right knee is on the ground, the opposite of the 1887 version. The person doing the technique is looking straight down as opposed to looking to his right at his toes.

手解 Tehodoki: Freeing Your Hands 8/12
両手返 Ryote Kaeshi: Two-Handed Reverse

両手返 リャウテカヘシ

○此手モ前ハ仝シク双方膝ニ手ヲ置キテ

對坐シ甲ノ方ヨリ「アイヤ」ト声掛ケ乙ノ

右ノ手首ヲ両手ニテ圖ノ如ク唯握ル

乙ノ方ハ「アイ」ト答ヘテ其持レタル手ノ

指先ヲ延べテ一寸許甲ノ左リノ膝ノ

向ヘ突キ出シ直ニ我カ左リ肩ロノトコロマデ引上

ケ持返シ手ノ掌ヲ逆ニナシテ又甲ノ元ノ

膝ノ脇横ヘ「アイ」ト声掛ケ押返スナリ

左右共ニ同シ理ナリ

乙　　甲

136

両手返 Ryote Kaeshi: Two-Handed Reverse

This technique begins the same way as the previous technique, with both you and the attacker seated in Seiza, facing each other with your hands on your knees.

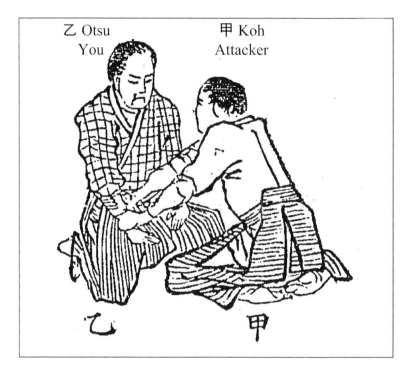

With a Kake-goe of *Eiya!* The Attacker grabs your right wrist with both hands. This is shown in the illustration. In response you should shout a Kake-goe of *Ya-a!* and put all your power in the fingertips of the hand the Attacker has seized. Thrust it slightly forward, towards the Attacker's left knee, then immediately yank your hand up over your left shoulder. Reverse your palm then, with a Kake-goe of *Eiya!* whip your arm down towards the Attacker's knees.

The left and right sides follow the same principle.

Ryote Dori (Ryote Kaeshi) from the 1893 edition

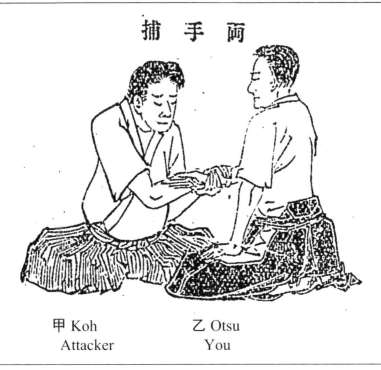

捕 手 両

甲 Koh
Attacker

乙 Otsu
You

Ryote Dori (Ryote Kaeshi) from the 1926 edition

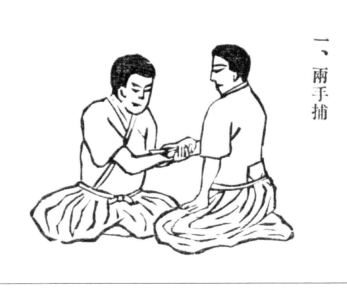

一、両手捕

Note:

Both the 1893 and the 1926 editions call this technique Ryote Dori, Two Handed Capture. However, judging by the illustration and the fact that it is listed after Kote Gaeshi and before Kidori (the following technique) it is the same technique.

The description from the 1893 edition also has some noticeable differences:

The Attacker grabs your right wrist with both hands, grabbing first with the right and then the left. In response the Attacker shifts his right knee back and pulls. You anticipate this action and suddenly stab your right hand forward then immediately yank it upward so your hand is above the Attacker's right wrist. Ensure you stab your fingers almost to the Attacker's waist.

手解 Tehodoki: Freeing Your Hands 9/12
気捕 Kidori: Seizing the Chance

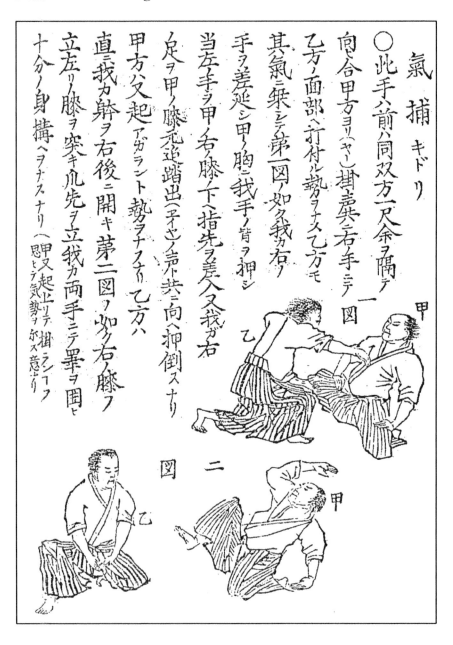

氣　捕　キドリ

○此手ハ前ノ双方二尺余ヲ隔テ一

向合甲方ヨリ（ャシ）掛来ル右手ニテ一図

乙方ノ面部へ打付ル勢ヲナス乙方モ

其氣ニ架シテ第一図ノ如ク我カ右ノ

手ヲ差延シ甲ノ胸ニ我手ノ皆ヲ押シ

当左手ヲ甲ノ右膝ノ下ヨリ指先ヲ差入ス又我ガ右

足ヲ甲ノ膝元ニ踏出（ヲセ）ノ声ト共ニ向へ押倒スナリ

甲方父起（アガラント勢ヲナスナリ乙方ハ

直ニ我カ躰ヲ右後ニ開キ第二図ノ如ク右ノ膝ヲ

立左リノ膝ヲ突キ爪先ヲ立我カ両手ニテ罡ノ囲ヒ

十分ノ身構へヲナスナリ（娶又起止リテ掛ヘシフ

（慰ヒテ氣勢ヲナス意ナリ

気捕 Kidori: Seizing the Chance

This technique begins the same way as the previous technique. Both you and the Attacker are seated facing each other in Seiza approximately 1 Shaku, 30 centimeters, apart.

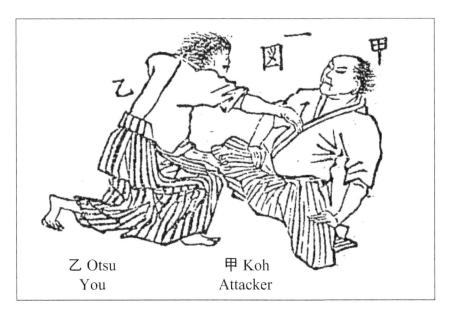

乙 Otsu   甲 Koh
You   Attacker

With a Kake-goe of *Yaa!* the Attacker shows his intention to punch you in the face with his right hand. Realizing this, you do as shown in illustration 1 (above.) Extend your right arm out and push the attacker in the chest with the back of your hand and, at the same time, slip the fingers of your left hand under his right knee.

乙 Otsu
You

甲 Koh
Attacker

    With a Kake-goe of *Eiya!* flip the attacker backwards. If the attacker seems like he is going to recover and attack, then you should rotate your body to the right and away so you are at an angle to the Attacker. As illustration 2 (above) shows, your right knee is upright while your left knee is planted on the ground with the toes of that foot on the ground and your heel off the ground. Both hands are held low surrounding your testicles and you are in a stable and ready stance. You should be vigilant against any attempt by the Attacker.

The final image of both the 1893 and 1926 editions show the arms forcefully extended.

1893 edition

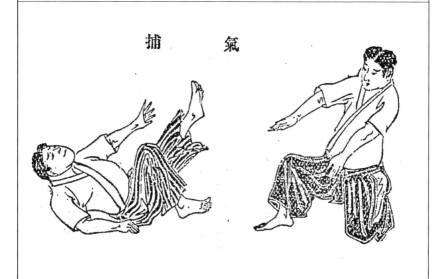

1926 edition

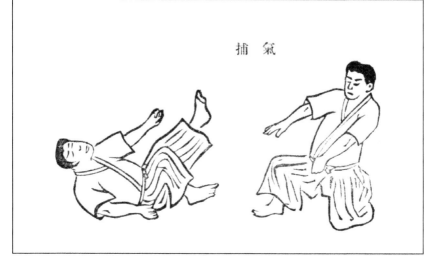

手解 Tehodoki: Freeing Your Hands 10/12
天倒 Tento: Top of the Head

天　倒　テントウ

○此手モ前ニ同シ双方向ヒ合膝ニ
手ヲ置ニ尺余ヲ隔坐シ居甲方ヨリ
徐ト掛ル声共ニ一図ノ如ク左ノ足ヲ乙ノ
膝ノ元ニ迫踏出シ乙ヲ両手ニテ抱込ム乙方ハ

（ヤ）答ヘ両手ニテ我筆ヲ囲ヒ作腰ヲ少シク
延上リ右足ヲ右ヘ開キ立膝ヲナシ左足膝ヲ
突ヲ兀先ヲ立テ我カ両肘ヲ張ル此時甲ノ抱込タル
双手ノスクが故ニ左ノ手ニテ甲ノ衣類ノ紋所ヲ掴
ミ右ノ手ヲ我カ肩ヘ引敨出シ甲ノ天倒ヘ拳ニテ
（俗ニグミ）押当（エイヤト言ッテ打落スナリ即チ二図
如ク拳ヲ強ヨク下ヘ押付ルナリ

一図
甲
乙

二図
乙
甲

天倒 Tento: Top of the Head

This technique begins the same way as the previous one. You and the Attacker are seated in Seiza across from each other, approximately 2 Shaku, 60 centimeters apart.

Illustration 1

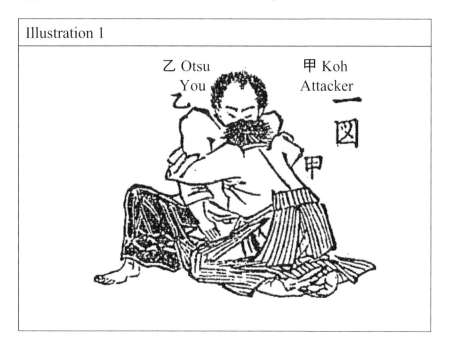

With a Kake-goe of Ei! The Attacker slides his left knee towards your knees and wraps his arms around you from the front. This is shown in illustration 1.

Illustration 2

You respond to this with a Kake-goe of *Yaa!* and bring both hands low, surrounding your testicles as you raise your hips up slightly and step out to the right with your right foot. Keep your left knee planted on the ground but stand up on your toes, with your heel off the ground. Put power in both elbows and push out. This will cause some space to form between you and the Attacker. Slip your left hand under the Attacker's right arm and around his back. Grip the Mon-dokoro, family crest, on the back of his shirt with your left hand. Raise your right shoulder up and free it from the Attacker's left arm, then plant your right fist on the Kyusho Tento, the top of his head.

This spot is also known colloquially as Gunkotsu, the soldier's bone. With a Kiai, another word for Kake-goe, of *Eiya!* knock him down. As is shown in illustration 2 use your fist to strongly push the attacker down.

Note: The illustrations on the following page combine the illustrations from the 1887 edition and the 1893 edition to give more complete picture of the technique.

Illustration 1 1887

Illustration 2 1893

Illustration 3 1887

手解 Tehodoki: Freeing Your Hands 11/12
扱捕 Mogi Dori: Plucking Away

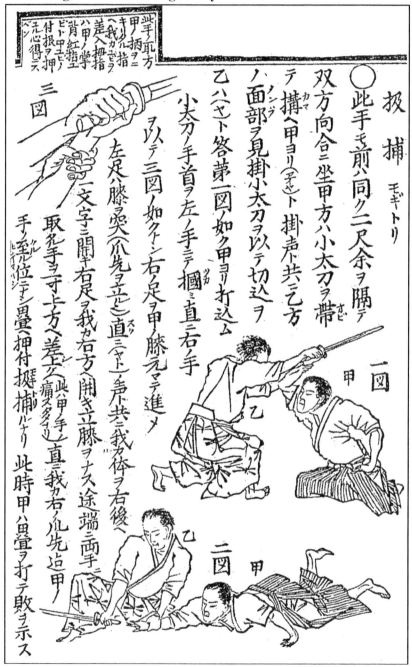

扱捕 Mogi Dori: Plucking Away

This technique begins the same way as the previous technique with both combatants seated in Seiza facing each other approximately 2 Shaku, 60 centimeters apart.

乙 Otsu
You

甲 Koh
Attacker

The attacker draws a Kodachi short sword from his belt and goes into a ready to attack position. He then does a Kake-goe of *Eiya!* indicating he is preparing to cut down on the top of your head. As he begins his cut, respond with a Kake-goe of *Ya!* and, in one motion, grab the Attacker's right wrist with your left hand. Immediately grab the fingers holding the handle with your right hand.

Step forward and plant your right foot in front of the attacker's knees while keeping your left knee on the ground. The toes of your left foot should be on the ground with your heel off the ground. This is shown in illustration 1 (above.)

The detail illustration shows how to grip with the right hand.

Detail Illustration Text:

Dig your fingers under the fingers of the attacker holding the handle of his sword. Your thumb should be pushing at where the index finger and middle finger meet the back of the hand.

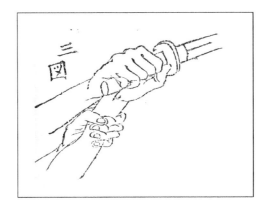

Immediately do a Kake-goe of *Yato!* and drop back with your right foot, turning your body completely sideways so you are making an Ichi-monji, a straight line like the Kanji for the number one 一. As you begin moving your right foot out to the side, raise your arms up a little. This will make the next step less painful for the Attacker. While moving your right foot, drag his arm towards the toes of your right foot. Pull the Attacker's arm down flat to the tatami so he releases his sword. This is Mogi Tori, Plucking Away. This is shown in illustration 2 (below.) The Attacker should slap the Tatami to signify his loss.

乙 Otsu
You

甲 Koh
Attacker

Step 1 from the 1893 Edition

Step 2 from the 1887 Edition

Step 3 from the 1926 Edition

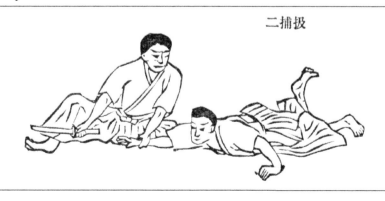

手解 Tehodoki: Freeing Your Hands 12/12
打手 Uchi Te: Striking Hand

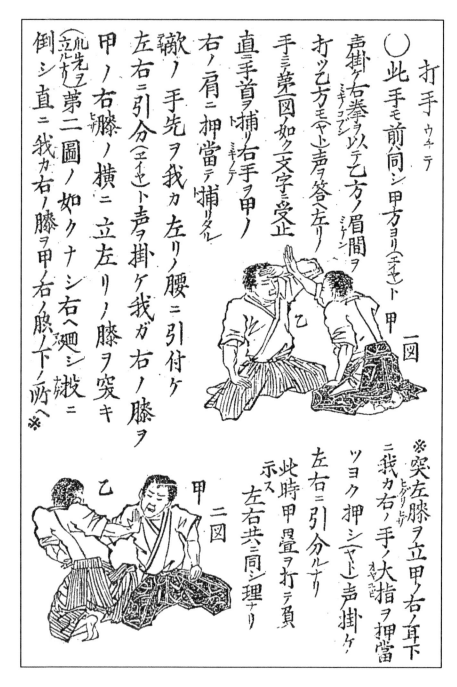

打手 Uchi Te: Striking Hand

This technique begins the same as the previous one.

1	2
乙 Otsu　　甲 Koh You　　Attacker	乙 Otsu　　甲 Koh You　　Attacker

The Attacker shouts a Kake-goe of *Eiya!* and punches to Miken, between your eyebrows. You respond with a Kake-goe of *Yato!* and do an Ichimonji block as shown in illustration 1 (left.) When doing an Ichimonji block your arm forms a straight line like the Kanji for the number one 一. Then immediately grab the Attacker's right wrist with your left hand.

With your right hand, slap down hard on the Attacker's right shoulder and grab. Next, pull the Attacker's right hand down to your left hip. With a Kake-goe of *Eiya!* plant your right foot beside the Attacker's right knee, push with your right hand and pull with your left. Your left knee is planted on the ground with the toes of your left foot on the ground and your heel off the ground.

As the second illustration (right) shows, topple the opponent onto his right side by rotating to the left. As you do this drop your right knee to the ground beside the Attacker's right armpit and stand on your left foot. Use your right thumb to press firmly just below the ear of the Attacker. Push with your right hand and pull with your left hand as you shout a Kake-goe of *Yato!* The attacker should slap the Tatami to indicate he has been defeated. The left and right sides of this technique are done the same.

初段 Shodan: First Level Techniques

真之位 Shin no Kurai: True Stance 1/10

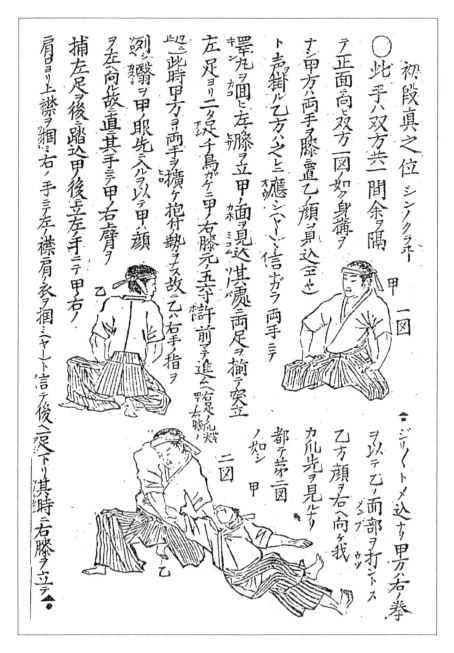

真之位 Shin no Kurai: True Stance

This technique begins with you and the Attacker seated in Seiza facing each other one Kan, or 180 centimeters, apart.

The Attacker, with his hands on his knees glares at you and shouts a Kake-goe of *Eiya!* you and the Attacker glare at each other and you respond with a Kake-goe of *Yaa!* as you press your right knee into the ground and step out to the left with your hands encircling your groin. This is shown in the first illustration.

From there, bring your feet together and stand up. Starting with your left foot take two rapid steps towards the Attacker. These steps should be quick like the Chidori, Japanese plover bird, with one foot crossing over the other. Your right foot should stop 5 or 6 Sun, 15-18 centimeters from the attacker's right knee.

The toes of your right foot should be near the Attacker's right knee. In response to this, the Attacker spreads his arms wide open as if to wrap you up. In response you bring the fingers of your right hand together and stab at the Attacker's eyes in order to obscure his vision and distract him. This will cause him to look away to the left. Use this distraction to grab the Attacker's upper arm and step behind him with your left foot.

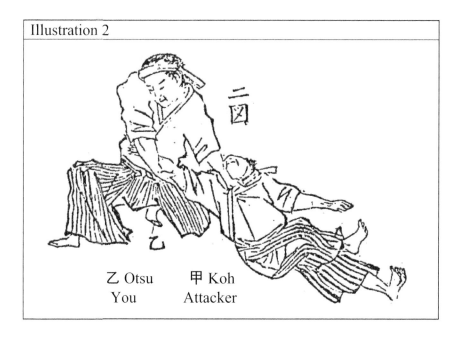

二図

乙 Otsu　　甲 Koh
You　　　　Attacker

With your left hand grab the Attacker's left upper collar. Your right hand should grab the collar, shoulder or some part of the sleeve.

Note: The illustration seems to show the right hand holding the elbow, or the end of the shirt sleeve.

With a *Yaa!* drop back one step with you left leg and plant your left knee. Keeping your right knee upright, use steady pressure to topple the Attacker.

The Attacker will ball up his left fist and try to punch you in the face so protect yourself by turning your head to the right and fix your gaze on the toes of your right foot. This is shown in illustration 2.

Differences in the 1926 Edition
In the first illustration (top) you keep your left foot close beside your right foot .
In the second illustration you are holding the Attacker's right wrist.

位之眞 、一

眞ノ位二圖

初段 Shodan: First Level Techniques 2/10
添捕 Soe-dori: Alongside Seizure

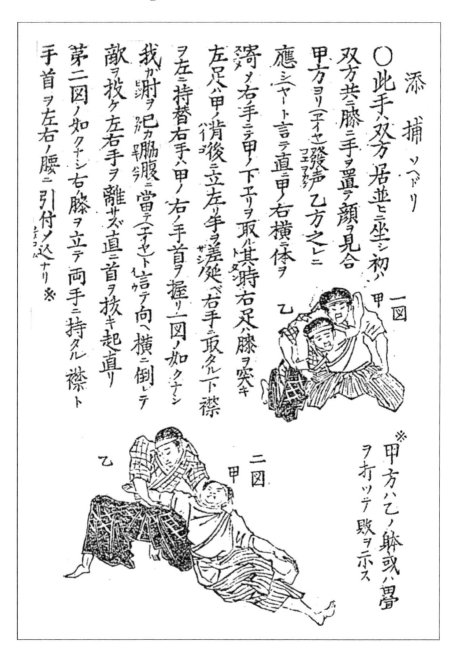

添捕 Soe-dori: Alongside Seizure

This technique begins with both combatants seated in Seiza alongside each other, with their hands on their knees.

You and the Attacker turn to look at each other and the Attacker shouts a Kake-goe of *Eiya!* In response to this you shout a Kake-goe of *Yaato!* and immediately shift your body towards the Attacker's right knee. You then grab the Attacker's lower lapel with your right hand, as you do this press your right knee into the ground and step behind him with your left foot.

The Attacker responds by wrapping his right arm across the Attacker's back and around his neck towards where your right hand grips. Grab his right collar with your left hand and release with your left hand.

With a Kake-goe of Eiya! Topple the Attacker beside you by pulling both your elbows into your sides. You should not release your left and right hands while throwing, however you should immediately free your head and end up in the position shown in illustration 2.

Note: It seems like you free your head after your right and left hands are in position.

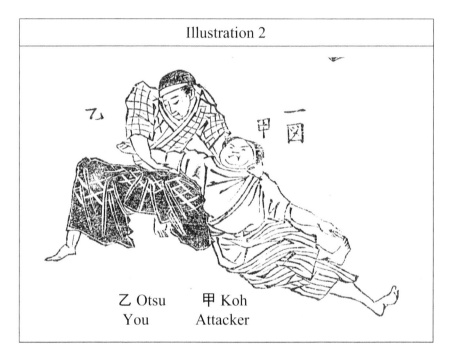

Illustration 2

乙 Otsu   甲 Koh
You   Attacker

Your right leg is upright and both the left hand griping the Attacker's collar and the right hand gripping the wrist should be pulled to your waist. The Attacker strikes the tatami mat or his body to indicate he is defeated.

Note: The following page shows Alongside Siezure with images from the 1926 edition included. These images show slightly different stages of the technique.

初段 Shodan: First Level Techniques 3/10
御前捕 Gozen Dori: Before Royalty Technique

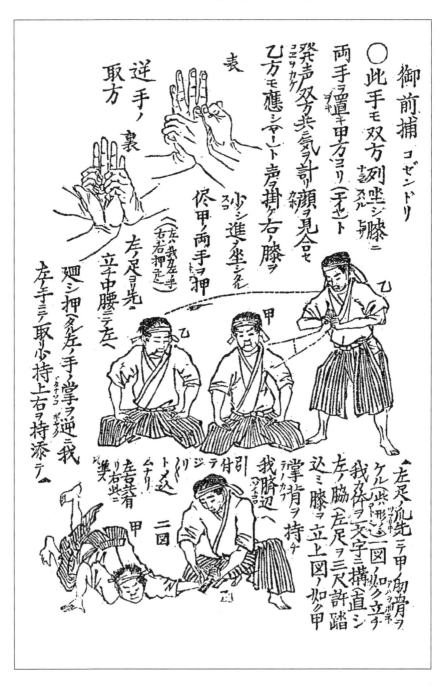

御前捕 Gozen Dori: Before Royalty Technique

This technique also begins with both combatants seated in Seiza beside each other, with their hands on their knees.

Illustration 1

乙 Otsu You   甲 Koh Attacker   乙 Otsu You

The Attacker shouts a Kake-goe of *Eiya!* locks eyes with you. You stare at each other and seek to judge each other's intentions. You respond with a Kake-goe of *Yaa!* and move your right knee forward so it is approximately 20 centimeters in front of the Attacker.

Press your right hand on top of the Attacker's right hand and then place your left hand on top of his left hand. The thumb of your left hand should be on the back of his left hand and you should allow your fingers to wrap around the far side of his palm. Bring your left leg up beside your right leg and stand up in Nakagoshi, standing with hips low to the ground.

Detail Illustration:
Gyaku Te no Torikata
How to take the wrist lock. Right image shows how the fingers
are placed on the back of the hand. The left from the palm

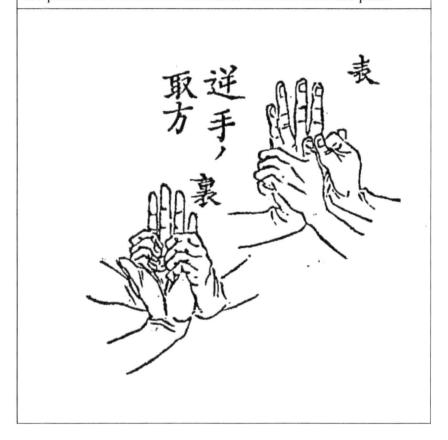

Release the Attacker's right hand as you rotate to your left and reverse the Attacker's left hand so his palm is facing away from you. Raise the hand up at the same time. Bring your right hand up to join your left hand as shown in the detail illustration.

With the toes of your left foot, kick the Attacker in the ribs. This kick should not actually strike your training partner during practice. It should just show Katachi, the movement. This is all shown in illustration 1.

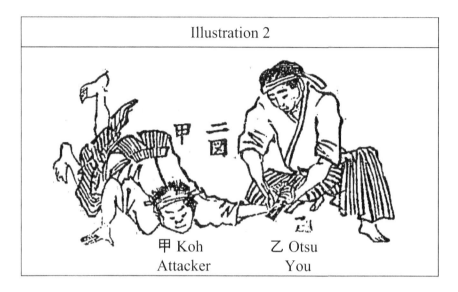

Illustration 2
甲 Koh   乙 Otsu Attacker   You

Step out sideways to the left about 3 Shaku, 90 centimeters, with your left foot and drop down onto your right knee. Be sure to keep hold of the Attacker's left hand and pull it towards your navel as shown in illustration 2. Apply steady pressure to the wrist. The left and right sides of this technique are done the same way.

1926 Edition Illustration 1

御前捕一

1926 Edition Illustration 2

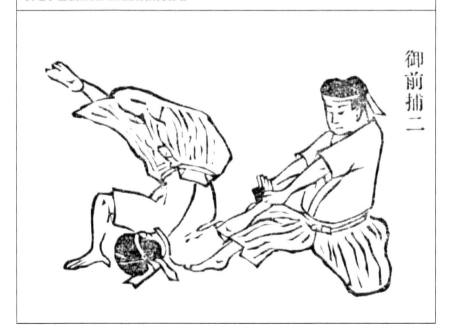

御前捕二

Note:

Both the 1893 and 1926 editions handle the end of Before Royalty Technique differently. After taking the Attacker's left wrist in a lock, you kick with your left foot to the Attacker's ribs. You then pull that leg back, dropping onto your left knee and keeping your right leg upright.

As you drop back keep your arms straight in order to keep pressure on the arm. In the end the Attacker's wrist should be by your right knee. The Attacker should do Ukemi, or roll out at the end.

初段 Shodan: First Level Techniques 4/10
袖車 Sode Guruma: Sleeve Wheel

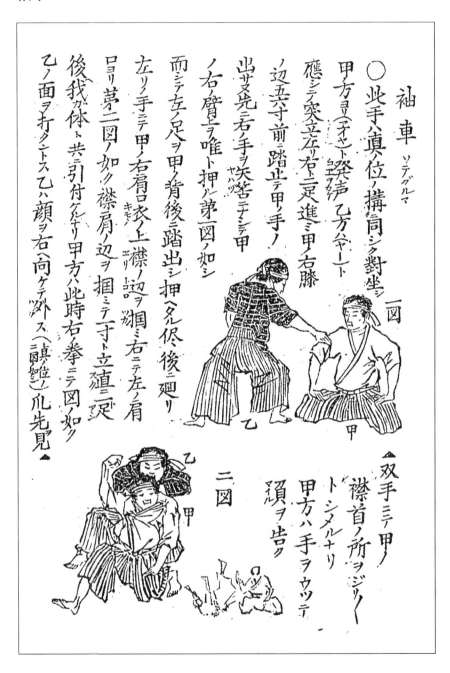

袖車 Sode Guruma: Sleeve Wheel

This technique begins in the same way as Shin noKurai, True Stance, with both you and the Attacker seated in Seiza across from each other with your hands on your knees.

Illustration 1

乙 Otsu
Attacker

甲 Koh
You

The Attacker shouts Eiya! You respond with Yaa! and stand up. Starting with your left foot take two quick steps towards the Attacker, stopping 5 or 6 Sun, 15~18 centimeters, in front of his right knee. Before the Attacker can react, shape your right hand into a Yahazu, nock of an arrow, and shove the right upper arm of the Attacker. This is shown in illustration 1.

Next, step behind the Attacker with your left foot and position yourself behind him. With your left hand reach over the Attacker's right shoulder and grab somewhere around his front collar. Then, with your right hand, reach over his left shoulder and grab somewhere around the collar on that side. This is shown in illustration 2.

Illustration 2 (Plus bonus sketch)

Raise yourself up slightly before stepping backwards begin sure to hold tightly so the attacker will be pulled backwards.

As the Attacker is pulled backwards he attempts to punch you in the face with his right fist. Turn your head to the left and look at the toes of your left foot to avoid this strike. This is shown in illustration 2 and is also similar to the second illustration of the first technique in the Shodan, First Level Technique, True Stance. Work both hands to slowly increase pressure on the attacker's neck. The Attacker should tap to show he is defeated.

Note: Adding the illustrations from the 1926 (illustrations 2 & 3) edition, as well as the sketech by an unknown previous owner of this book, makes the sequence easier to visualize.

初段 Shodan: First Level Techniques 5/10
飛違 Tobi Chigai: Leaping In and Attacking (Reversing the Situation)

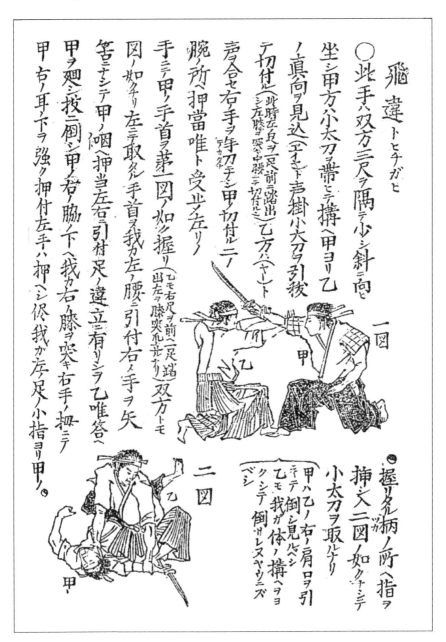

飛違 Tobi Chigai: Leaping In and Attacking (Reversing the Situation)

This technique begins with both combatants seated in Seiza 3 Shaku, 90 centimeters, apart. The Attacker is slightly angled away from you and has a Kodachi, short sword, in his belt.

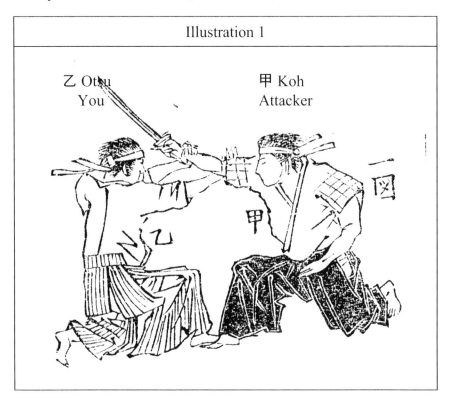

Illustration 1

The Attacker turns his gaze on you and, with a Kake-goe of *Eiya!* draws his Kodachi and cuts to the top of your head. When doing this the Attacker steps forward with his right foot and plants his left knee on the ground. He is cutting from a position known as Nakagoshi, or middle hips. You match the Attacker's shout with a Kake-goe of *Yaa!* and, forming your right hand into a Shuto or Tegatana strike the upper arm of the Attacker's sword arm. This will stop his arm. With your left hand seize the Attacker's right wrist. When striking his arm, you should step forward with your right foot and plant your left knee on the ground. This is all shown in illustration 1.

Illustration 2

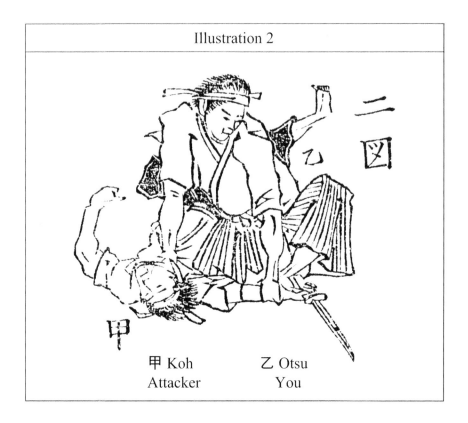

甲 Koh　　　　乙 Otsu
Attacker　　　　You

Keeping a grip on the Attacker's right wrist, bring your left hand down to your waist. Form your right hand into a Ya-hazu (nock of an arrow shape) and grab the Attacker's throat and push. Pulling on his wrist and pushing on his throat allows you to topple the Attacker to your left. As you do this, drop your right knee down beside the Attacker's left ribcage and stand up on your left foot. With the thumb of your right hand press firmly just below the ear while holding the Attacker's right wrist securely.

Use the toes of your left foot to push the sword hand out of the Attacker's grip. This is shown in illustration 2.

Note: This could also mean "Wedge your toes under the handle of the sword."

After being thrown the Attacker attempts to drag you down to the side by grabbing your right sleeve. Make sure you are well positioned in order to prevent this.

Illustration 1 & 2 from the 1893 version

一　遶　飛

甲 Koh
Attacker

乙 Otsu
You

二　遶　飛

甲 Koh
Attacker

乙 Otsu
You

初段 Shodan: First Level Techniques 6/10
抜身目付 Nukimi Metsuke: Locking Eyes and Drawing

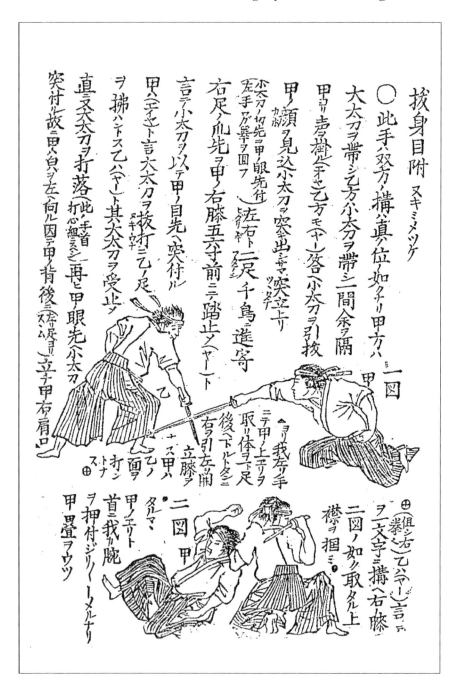

抜身目付 Nukimi Metsuke: Locking Eyes and Drawing

This technique begins from the same position as shown in the first technique of the Shodan, Shin no Kurai. Both you and the Attacker are seated in Seiza 1 Kan apart. (One Kan is 6 Shaku or 180 centimeters.) Your eyes are locked. The Attacker has an O-Dachi, Large Tachi while you have a Kodachi, short sword in your belt. The Attacker has his left hand on the scabbard of his sword while your hands are both resting on your knees.

Note: The author uses O-Dachi and Ko-Dachi to describe the long and short swords worn by a Samurai. They can also be referred to as Daito and Shoto. Typically "Tachi" describes the large swords that hung blade down from the hip by straps which Samurai mounted on horseback wore in the Warring States Era. The 1926 version of this book states that the blade should be 3 Shaku and 2 Sun, or 96 centimeters in length.

1. Tachi
2. O-Dachi, long sword, more commonly known as Dai-to.
3. Ko-Dachi, short sword, more commonly known as Sho-to.
4. Tanto- Knife

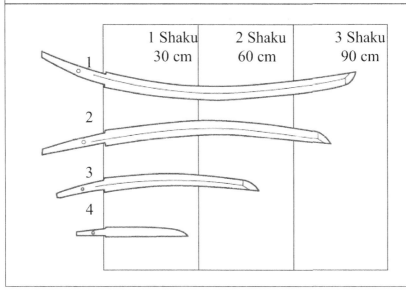

The technique starts when the Attacker shouts a Kake-goe of Eiya! And you respond with your own Kake-goe of Ya! while moving your right hand to the handle of your sword, being careful not to grip too tightly. Draw your sword in a smooth, clean motion and end up with your arm and sword forming a straight line from your shoulder to the Kisaki, tip of the blade. Aim the Kisaki at the Attacker's left eye.

The first illustration in the 1922 version shows the image after you draw your Ko-Dachi

一、

抜身目附一

Extend your arms towards the Attacker's eye as you take two quick steps forward, like the Chidori bird, stopping 5 or 6 Sun, 15-18 centimeters, in front of the Attacker's right knee.

Note: The 1922 version says to stop 7 or 8 Sun 21-24 centimeters.

Illustration 1

乙 Otsu — You

甲 Koh — Attacker

Shout a Kake-goe of *Yaa!* and stab your Ko-Dachi towards the Attacker's eyes. The Attacker responds with a Kake-goe of *Eiya!* and, in one motion, draws his O-Dachi and cuts across your right leg. Respond with a Kake-goe of *Yaa!* and block and stop the Attacker's cut with your Ko-Dachi. The best way to do this is to twist your hand so your pinky is up, thereby rotating the blade downward. After stopping the cut, knock the Attacker's O-Dachi to the ground by deftly rotating the back of your hand around in a quick motion.

Immediately return your Kodachi to the Attacker's eyes and thrust forward. This will cause the Attacker to flinch to his left. Use this chance to step behind the Attacker, moving left foot first.

Reach over the Attacker's left shoulder and grab his right upper collar.

Note: The 1926 book has more detail: Grip with your thumb inside the collar and the other fingers outside.

Pull your right leg back and drop onto your left knee as you drag the Attacker back. The Attacker will attempt to punch you in the face with his right fist. Respond with a Kake-goe of *Yaa!* and take Ichimonji Kamae, make your body into a straight line, as shown in Illustration 2. With your left hand still holding the Attacker's collar drop your left forearm into the Attacker's neck and slowly increase pressure. The Attacker slaps the Tatami mat to indicate he is defeated.

初段 Shodan: First Level Techniques 7/10
鐺返 Kojiri Gaeshi: Reversing the Scabbard Cap

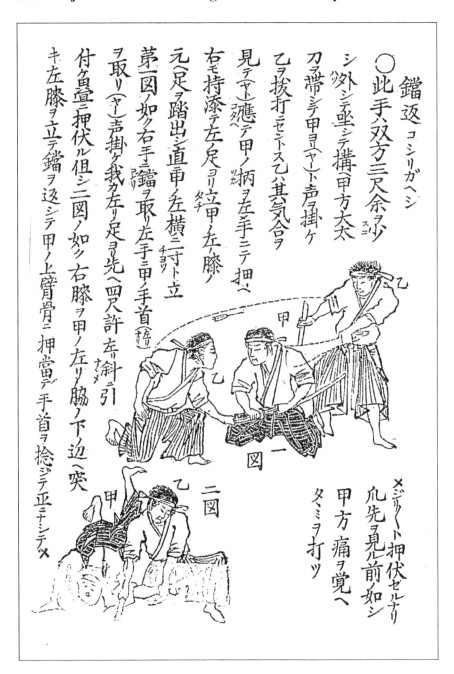

○此手ハ双方三尺余ヲ少

シ外シテ坐シテ構〈甲方大太

刀ヲ帯シテ甲ヨリ〈ヤ〉ト声ヲ掛ケ

乙ヲ抜打ニセントス乙其気合ヲ

見テ〈ヤト〉應テ甲ノ柄ヲ左ノ手ニテ押ヘ

右モ持添テ左ノ足ヨリ甲ノ左ノ膝ノ

元〈足ヲ踏出シ直甲ノ左横ニ付テ立

第一図ノ如ク右手ニ鐺ヲ取リ左ノ手ニ甲ノ手首〈掂〉

ヲ取リ〈ヤ〉声ヲ掛ケ我カ左ノ足ヲ先ヘ四尺許左ヘ斜ニ引

付ケ鼻畳ニ押伏ル但シ二図ノ如ク右膝ヲ甲ノ左ノ脇ノ下辺ヘ〈突

キ左ノ膝ヲ立テ鐺ヲ返シテ甲ノ上臂骨ニ押當テ手首ヲ捻ジテ正ニナシテメ

メジク〈ト押伏ゼルナリ

爪先ヲ見ル前ノ如シ

甲方ノ痛ヲ覚ヘ

タミヲ打ツ

鐺返 Kojiri Gaeshi: Reversing the Scabbard Cap

This technique begins with both combatants seated in Seiza 3 Shaku, 90 centimeters apart, facing slightly away from each other. The Attacker has an O-Dachi in his belt and his left hand on the scabbard.

Illustration 1

The Attacker first shouts a Kake-goe of *Yaa!* and shows his intention to do a Nuki-uchi, or draw and cut, attack on you by placing his right hand on the handle of his sword. Respond with a Kake-goe of *Yato!* and reach out and stop the handle of the Attacker's sword with your left hand. As you stand up on your right foot join your right hand to your left.

Step across so you are standing beside the Attacker's left knee. Next, do as shown in Illustration 1. Grab the Kojiri, end of the scabbard, of the Attacker's sword with your right hand and grab his left wrist with your left hand. With a Kake-goe of *Yaa!* step diagonally to the left, starting with your left foot approximately 4 Shaku, 120 centimeters, and pull the Attacker down. The Attacker should be pulled face down onto the Tatami mat.

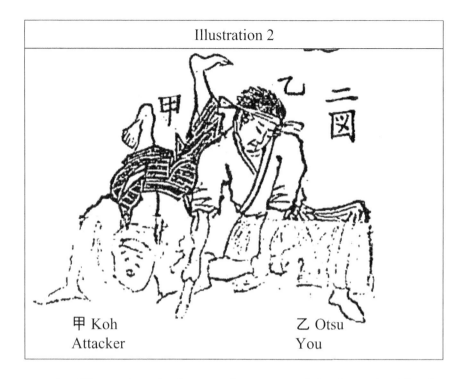

Illustration 2

甲 Koh
Attacker

乙 Otsu
You

As Illustration 2 shows, plant your right knee beside the Attacker's lower left side. Your left knee is upright and the Kojiri is pushed down so it presses into the back of his arm hard enough that you can feel the bone. You should bend the wrist into a lock and gradually increase the pressure. Just as in the other techniques you should end by looking at your toes. The attacker should strike the ground when he feels pain.

Note: Three cheers to the enterprising fellow, or lady, who re-illustrated the picture after it was torn off.

Adding the illustrations from the 1898 edition (Illustrations 2 & 3) makes the technique easier to visualize.

初段 Shodan: First Level Techniques 8/10
両手捕 Ryo-te Dori: Responding to a Two-Handed Attack

両手捕 リヤウテドリ

○此手ハ双方共三尺

余ヲ隔向と合膝ニ手ヲ

置キテ坐ス而シテ甲方

ヨリ（子イ）ト声ヲ掛ケ乙ノ両

手首ヲ取ル乙方ハ（ヱイ）ト應シ

其持ヒタル左右ノ手ヲ前ノ

振解ノ如ク我ガ左ノ肩先ニ引テ拂ハラヒ直ニ

甲ノ右肩ロノ衣類ヲ摑ミ又左手ヲ振掃ヒ甲ノ右手首ヲ取（乙ノ握ハタル手ヲ

（ヱイヤ）ト言サマ甲ノ右膝ノ横ニ寸ト立ツ此時ニ甲　右ノ肋骨ヲ一本跳込ム（祖形直

二我ガ真前ニ引付第二図ノ如ク捻伏セ右膝ヲ甲ノ上臂ニ押當テ左手ニ

取名甲ノ手首ヲ一文字ニ立テ膝ニテシリ／＼ト押付ルナリ

図一

乙　甲　二図

両手捕 Ryo-te Dori: Responding to a Two-Handed Attack

In this technique both you and the attacker are seated in Seiza facing each other with your hands on your knees.

乙 Otsu
You

甲 Koh
Attacker

The attacker shouts a Kake-goe of *Eiya!* and grabs both your wrists. You shout a Kake-goe of *Ei!* and free your right hand using the previously described Furi Hotoki. After yanking your right hand up to your left shoulder and thereby shaking off the attacker's grip, grab the fabric on his right shoulder. Next, shake off the attacker's right hand which is gripping your left wrist and take hold of his right wrist.

(Rotating your wrist around will allow you to easily free yourself from the attacker's grip.)

With a Kake-goe of *Eiya!* take a short step forward with your right foot so you are beside the attacker's right knee. Next, kick the attacker in the ribs on his right side. (This should be done "Katachi" or just show the motion without making contact.)

Note: Both the 1893 & 1926 editions show the kick as being with the right foot.

1893	1926

Illustration 2

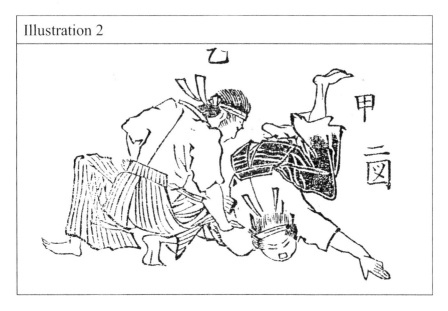

Then immediately pull him down in front of you as shown in illustration 2. After you twist the attacker onto the ground plant your right knee on the attacker's right arm just above his elbow. With your left hand twist the opponent's right wrist so his hand is straight up so it makes an Ichi Monji, the Kanji for one, as you use your right knee to grind into the back of his arm.

Combination sequence with the 1887 and 1893 editions

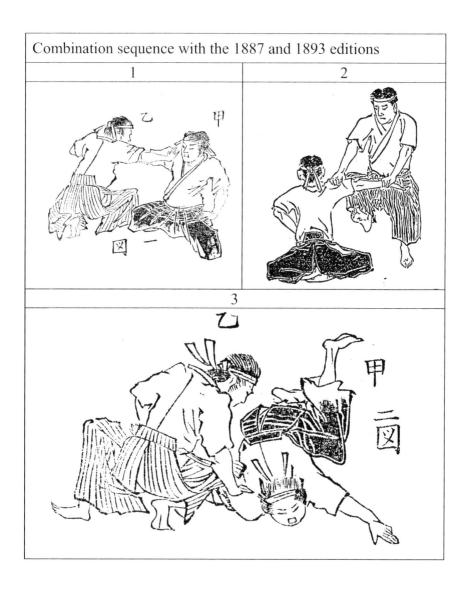

初段 Shodan: First Level Techniques 9/10
壁添 Kabe Soi: Pressed Against a Wall

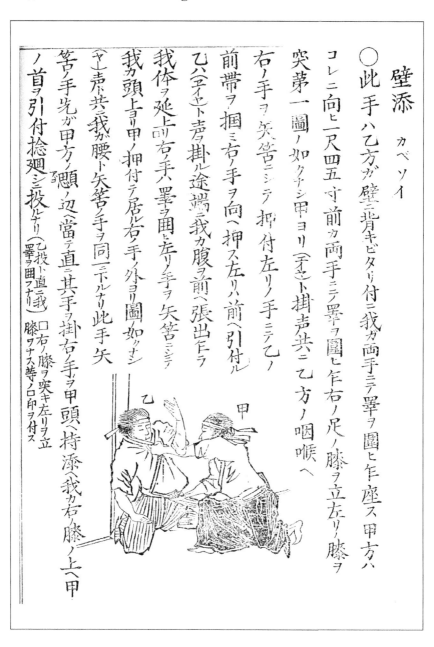

壁添 Kabe Soi: Pressed Against a Wall
Kabe Zoe: Against the Wall

In this technique you have your back flat against a wall. You are seated in Seiza with your arms hanging down and your hands are encircling your groin.

乙 Otsu   甲 Koh
You   Attacker

The attacker is seated 1.4 or 1.5 Shaku, 42~45 centimeters across from you with his hands circling his groin. With a Kake-goe of *Eiya!* the Attacker steps forward with his right foot while keeping his weight on his left knee. He forms his left hand into a Yahazu, nock of an arrow and grabs your throat. With his right hand he grabs your Obi, belt, from below. He pushes back with his left hand and pulls forward with his right.

You respond with a Kiai of Eiya! As you extend your stomach forward. At the same time, extend your body upward. When doing this keep your right knee on the ground and stand up on your left foot. Keeping your right hand around your groin, raise your left arm over your head and form your left hand into a Yahazu shape. This is shown in the illustration.

With your left hand, which is in Yahzu shape, strike the Attacker in the jaw and grab. With your right hand grab his head. Twist and pull his head down towards your right knee causing him to flip over. Once you finish the throw return your hands to the start position, surrounding your groin.

The instructions in the 1887 edition state the Attacker's right hand is grabbing the throat however the illustration clearly shows the left hand grabbing the throat. This was accounted for in the illustration and the instructions were changed to match the illustration.

Both the 1893 and the 1926 edition describe the Attacker's first move as being with the right hand.

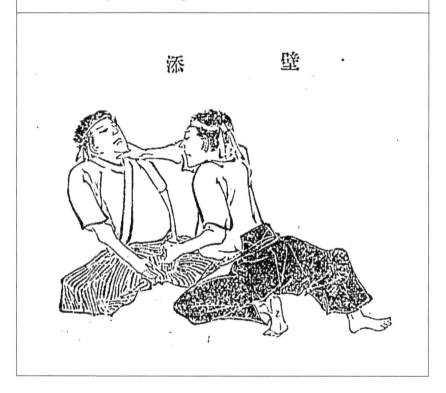

初段 Shodan: First Level Techniques 10/10
後捕 Ushiro Dori: Responding when Attacked from Behind

後捕 ウシロドリ

○此手ハ乙方ガ壁際ヨリ三尺余ヲ隔向ヲ廣ク 一図
明テ両手ニテ畧ヲ囲ヒ尓坐スナリ甲方ハ乙ノ後
ニ在リ(エイヤ)掛声ト共ニ左足ヲ立藤ヲナシ右ノ膝ヲ
突第一図ノ如ク乙ノ背後ヘ抱付ナリ乙ハ(ヤ)
答ノ声ト共ニ我ガ頭ノ頂ヲ甲ノ額ヘ当心ニナシ
(呷ルノ悟)我ガ躰ヲ少シ延上リ右ノ膝ヲ突左ヲ左ノ
後(足ヲ開キ(ヤ)ト声ヲ搤ルトタンニ我ガ両肘ヲ張ルト
甲ノ抱メタル手ノ弛ム故直ニ我ガ腰ヲ下ルタンニ二図ノ如ク 甲
右ノ手ニテ甲ノ右ノ肩ロノ衣類ヲ掴ミ左ノ手ニテ甲足ノ
脚踝ヲ押ハネル(エイヤ)ト言テ我ガ前ヘ右ニ掴ミタル手ヲ強ク 二図
引落ニ投ルナリ (乙ハ投ラルル片我ガ右ノ肩突コマヌ
(起直ニ我畧ヲ囲ヒ甲ノ後ニ(甲ハ投ラルル片我ガ右ノ肩突コマヌ
(ヤウ成可徐ケ投ラル心得ニスヘシ)

後捕 Ushiro Dori: Responding when Attacked from Behind

In this technique you are seated in Seiza, approximately 3 Shaku, 90 centimeters, away from the wall with your arms held wide and ready. Your hands are encircling your groin.

Illustration 1

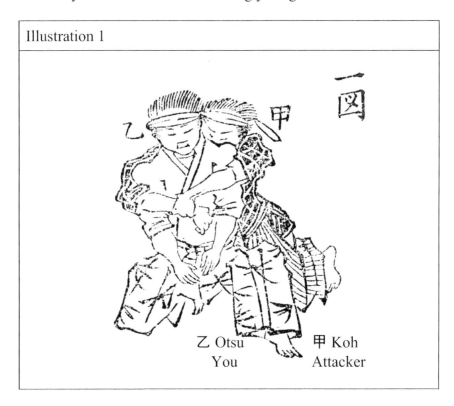

乙 Otsu
You

甲 Koh
Attacker

The opponent, who is seated behind you, shouts a Kake-goe of Eiya! Before pressing his right knee into the ground and standing up on his left foot and grabbing you from behind. This is shown in illustration 1.

You respond with a shout of *Yaa!* and whip your head back to strike the Attacker's forehead. The person in the role of the Attacker should turn his head to the left to avoid being struck during training.

Next, extend your body upward slightly by putting your weight on your right knee as you swing your left foot out to the left as you stand on it.

Illustration 2

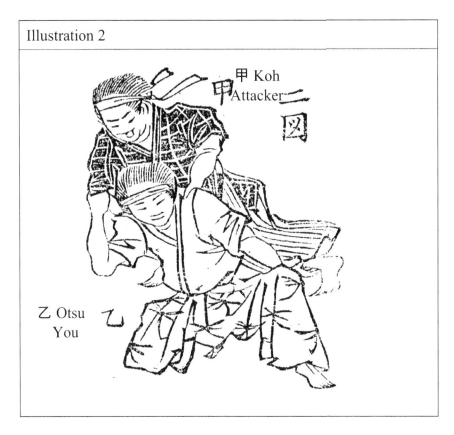

With a Kake-goe of *Yaa!* expand your elbows out in order to force off the Attacker's grip. As soon as you do this, grab the Attacker's shirt on his right shoulder with your right hand and push on the shin of his left foot with your left hand. With a Kake-goe of *Eiya!* pull down hard with your right hand, drop your hips down and throw the Attacker. This is shown in illustration 2.

Note: There are two notes in parenthesis, they are as follows:

After you finish the technique you should immediately return to a ready position, with your hands surrounding your groin and watching the Attacker for any signs of a counter attack.

During training the Attacker should be careful not to land hard on his right shoulder. You should be careful to throw the Attacker lightly.

Combination sequence with the 1887 and 1926 editions. The 1926 edition instructs you to stand up completely before dropping down onto your right knee.

End of Part One, 22 techniques.

Kenpo Zu

An Illustrated Guide to Kenpo

Copied by
Fujita Seiko

Date Unknown
Edo Era

Translator's Introduction

Image of a Tengu from 画図百鬼夜行 *The Illustrated Night Parade of a Hundred Demons.* Toriyama Sekien 1776

Kenpo Zu, An Illustrated Guide to Fighting, is a very mysterious book. It comprises of a series of 59 images of Tengu, mountain goblins, engaged in combat. Tengu are mythical teachers of martial arts. There is no information regarding the school of martial arts or the date *An Illustrated Guide to Fighting* was created. The illustrations were copied by Fujita Seiko (1898-1966,) the 14th heir to the Koga School of Ninjutsu and a famous martial arts researcher, from an unknown source. Each technique consists of a single image, likely serving as a reference for those who studied this school. Though there is no text in the book, the techniques seem to be divided into three categories:

- Jujutsu
- Muto-dori (unarmed against a sword)
- Dueling with Weapons. This can be Katana vs Katana, Katana vs Jutte (truncheon) or Katana vs Tessen (metal fan)

There are 32 Jujutsu techniques, 20 Muto-dori techniques and 7 Sword versus Jutte/Tessen techniques.

Jujutsu 31 Techniques	Muto-dori 21 Techniques

Dueling with weapons
7 Techniques

There are two types of Tengu shown in these illustration an avian type and a long-nosed type. There is a clear "winner" and "loser" in each technique and it is interesting to note that they alternate between each type of Tengu. This volume will introduce the Jujutsu from *An Illustrated Guide to Fighting* techniques along with some research regarding the origins of the Tengu.

Translator's Introduction to Tengu Part 1

Tengu are a type of Yokai, or supernatural being. The Kanji are literally "sky dog" which recalls the earlier Chinese meaning of the word, a constellation or a celestial event, such as a comet, that was considered a harbinger of ill fortune. In Japan, the first mention of Tengu as a celestial event was in the 8th century, however by the 12th century the Tengu were seen as mischievous spirits that led Buddhist and Zen monks astray, particularly those that were prideful or lazy. They also attempted to misdirect average people by pretending to be the Buddha.

Outline of the History of Tengu

The first mention of the Tengu is in the Nihon Shoki. It describes how in 637 AD a great comet appeared in the sky above the capital of Japan with an accompanying sound of thunder. Many perceived this as a harbinger of ill fortune. A monk by the name of Somin, who had just returned for a decade of Buddhist study in China wrote,

It is not a shooting star, rather it is a Tengu. Its howl is like thunder.

Chigiri Kosai, who published the comprehensive study Tengu no Kenkyu 1950, a collection of legends, trivia and appearances of Tengu in literature throughout Japanese history, makes some interesting comments.

"Somin was probably familiar with the word Tengu as it appears in many Chinese texts such as the *Classics of Mountains and Seas* (3~4th century BC,) *Records of the Grand Historian* (1st century BC,) *Book of Han* (1st century AD.) Other books showed Tengu looking like monkeys or birds, however the most of the history books described Tengu as celestial objects that portended ill fortune."

Tengu from *Classics of Mountains and Seas* (3~4th century BC.)

There is a considerable interval after Somin's reference to Tengu before the word again appears in literature. Chigiri Kosai notes, "In fact the (9th century) *Record of Miraculous Events in Japan: The Nihon Ryoiki* 本霊異記) does not contain an entry for Tengu despite covering spirit birds, spirit beasts, spirit fish and spirit insects…thus there doesn't seem to be any documents that show when or how the Tengu evolved from a celestial phenomenon to a kind of magical creature who resides in the mountains."

The next reference occurs some two centuries later in a single line from the early 11th century Tale of Genji, *Tengu are much like tree spirits.*

The *Torikaebaya Monogatari* とりかへばや物語, literally "If only I could exchange (them) ! story"), translated into English as *The Changelings*, by Unknown, (date unknown, written as early as the 8th century or as late as the 12th century) is the story of two nobles, a brother and a sister, who have a magic spell cast on them by a Tengu, which switches their genders, Making the male into female and the female into male." Chigiri Kosai feels this is the first example of the magical powers of the Tengu.

The big change comes with the publication of the 今昔物語集 *Anthology of Tales from the Past*, written in 1077, contains 11 stories about Tengu. The stories tend to follow the interactions of Tengu with wayward or corrupt Buddhist priests, but also how they attempt to deceive lay people as well. I have translated two of these to get a sense of how the Tengu were presented.

伊吹山の天狗と三修禅師

The Tengu and the Zen Priest Sanshu of Gokoku Temple on Ibuki Mountain

From: *Anthology of Tales from the Past*, written in 1077

Long ago, there was a Zen Priest Sanshu. Sanshu had set aside study of religious texts and instead devoted himself solely to Nenbutsu, the practice of mindfully chanting the name of Amitabha in order to ensure his rebirth into Sukhavati, the western paradise.

One day he heard a faint voice that seemed to emulate from the sky. It said, "Due to your diligent recitation of the Nenbutsu, I will lead you to paradise tomorrow afternoon. The Zen priest was so overjoyed that he cancelled his classes and sat chanting the Nenbutsu as he waited. Soon, from out of the west, a light shone and the face of the Buddha emerged, wreathed in gold light accompanied by the faint sounds of music.

A swirling purple cloud appeared around the priest and, taking the hand of Kannon he disappeared into the sky towards the west.

Seven days later as the student monks were gathering firewood when they discovered their teacher bound with vines to the top of a cedar tree. Though he was half-starved he continued to chant the Nenbutsu. The young monks were quite astounded and sought to rescue their teacher. However when they began to take him down he shouted, *Do not attempt to forestall my passage into the next realm!*

In the end they carried him home and lamented, *Our teacher has been deceived by a Tengu!*

The Zen priest never recovered his mind and after 3 more days of chanting the Nenbutsu he expired.

Note: This story seems to focus on a lack of learning and being insufficiently versed in literature.

天狗現仏坐木末語
The Tale of the Tengu that Manifested itself as a Buddha Atop a Tree
From: *Anthology of Tales from the Past*, written in 1077

This took place in the Enki Era 897-930 during the reign of Emperor Daigo. In the Gojo section of Kyoto an apparition of the Buddha appeared on the top of a persimmon tree, emanating a beautiful golden light. Innumerable people gathered about to gawk and revel in the splendor of the Buddha. Soon the crowds had swelled to the point horses and palanquins could no longer pass. Prince Fukakusa (810-850) who later became Emperor Ninmyo, who was so renowned for his scholarship that he was known as the minister of Brightness thought something was awry. Why would the Buddha appear at the top of a tree? This may well someone using Genjutsu, the art of illusion.

Prince Fukakusa stood at the base of the tree and locked eyes with the apparition of the Buddha. In the treetop he saw a Buddha with light emanating from gold eyes causing beautiful flowers to rain down as if from heaven. The crowd was awed and stared reverently at the majestic display. However Prince Fukakusa continued to stare coolly and without blinking at the apparition. The staring contest continued for more than two hours. The prince did not sense any heart or spirit from the figure and the fall of flowers gradually ebbed. Soon after the true nature of the Buddha began to reveal itself as a giant black kite. It fell from the tree to the ground batting its wings and writhing. Some nearby ruffians, realizing they had been deceived, grabbed the kite, ripped its wings off and beat it to death.

Note: Persimmon trees can live for more than a hundred years, longer than people so they are thought to have mystical powers.

In the Kamakura Era 1185-1333 a book of Buddhist parables called 沙石集 *Sand and Pebbles* contains a lesson about Tengu,

You sometimes hear of Shingon Priests becoming Tengu. Afterward they become privy to great secrets and teach them to their students. So there are good Tengu and bad Tengu.

The Tale of the Heike 平家物語 (compiled prior to 1330) which tells of the Genpei war describes Tengu in detail,

Though they appear human they are not, though they seem bird-like they are not birds and though they may resemble a dog they are not dogs. The head is that of a dog, the hands and feet are human and it flies with two wings attached to its back.

In the 14th century there were several stories of Tengu teaching martial arts, particularly sword fighting, to Samurai. In the scene below the Samurai Minamoto no Yoshitsune is receiving marital arts training from two Tengu, an avian Tengu and a long nosed more human-looking Tengu. The long nose relates to Tengu's desire to punish arrogance and prejudice in both priests and laymen.

The Tengu on the right holding a Ha-Uchiwa, fan made of feathers, is Sojobo a mountain hermit, who is said to be the "high Buddhist priest" of Tengu.

In the mid to late Edo Era 1700-1868, Tengu began to be seen as protectors of mountains and forests. For example people would hear a loud noise in the forest and run to see what the disturbance

was. There they would find a great tree had fallen. It was called Tengu Taoshi 天狗倒し "Felled by a Tengu." Tengu were also said to make rocks fall from the sky in order to chase trespassers off their mountain in what was called Tengu Tsubute 天狗飛礫 "Rocks thrown by a Tengu." Sometimes travelers in the mountains would hear the sound of many people laughing, this was called Tengu Warai 天狗笑い Tengu's Laugh. When staying overnight in a small mountain hut Tengu Yusuri 天狗ゆすり, or Tengu's Shake would cause the hut to shudder.

Today they are generally seen as benevolent if mischievous creatures and are more closely aligned with Kami, native Japanese Shinto gods.

End of Introduction to Tengu Part 1

**Kenpo Zu
An Illustrated Guide to Kenpo
Part 1: Jujutsu (31 Techniques)**

Copied by
Fujita Seiko

Date Unknown
Edo Era

End of A Curious Collection of Jujutsu Manuals Volume 2

Printed in Great Britain
by Amazon

82242169R00129